CEO Guide to Doing Business in Brazil

By Ade Asefeso MCIPS MBA

Second Edition

ISBN-13: 978-1499542516

ISBN-10: 1499542518

Publisher: AA Global Sourcing Ltd
Website: http://www.aaglobalsourcing.com

Table of Contents

Disclaimer

This publication is designed to provide competent and reliable information regarding the subject matter covered. However, it is sold with the understanding that the author and publisher are not engaged in rendering professional advice. The authors and publishers specifically disclaim any liability that is incurred from the use or application of contents of this book.

If you purchased this book without a cover you should be aware that this book may have been stolen property and reported as "unsold and destroyed" to the publisher. In this case neither the author nor the publisher has received any payment for this "stripped book."

Dedication

This book is dedicated to the hundreds of thousands of incredible souls in the world who have weathered through the up and down of recent recession.

To my family and friends who seems to have been sent here to teach me something about who I am supposed to be. They have nurtured me, challenged me, and even opposed me.... But at every juncture has taught me!

This book is dedicated to my lovely boys, Thomas, Michael and Karl. Teaching them to manage their finance will give them the lives they deserve. They have taught me more about life, presence, and energy management than anything I have done in my life.

Chapter 1: Introduction

Even for the seasoned exporter, Brazil is a tough proposition due to the procedures that need to be followed. This book is aimed at companies experienced in overseas trade who are new to doing business with Brazil. You may be an exporter looking to sell directly to Brazilian customers or through an agent or distributor in Brazil. Alternatively, you may be planning to set up a representative office, joint venture or other form of permanent presence in Brazil.

This book aims to provide a route map of the way ahead, together with signposts to other sources of help. It identifies the main issues associated with initial research, market entry, risk management, cultural and language issues. It also includes questions you should ask at the beginning of your research into Brazil.

The objective of this book is to steer companies through the initial research and preparation stages of entering the Brazilian market. It is far better to spend time and money carrying out thorough research and preparation before entering the market than to enter Brazil in a rush, only to discover, when it is too late, that you have made a poor and expensive decision!

This book is not designed to be read from cover to cover, but more as a useful reference to dip in and out of. The book will take you through the process of doing business in Brazil.

Brazil is simply too big a market to ignore. It is the fifth-largest country in the world, with a population of approximately 190 million. It has one of the world's most rapidly developing economies and a GDP per head that is greater than either India or China. It has natural resources in abundance, a developed industrial base, high standards in scientific research and substantial human capital.

Brazil is one of the four countries which, together with Russia, India and China, make up the so-called BRIC economies. The term was first used in 2001 by the investment bank Goldman Sachs which highlighted the huge potential of Brazil and recognised that, together with the other BRIC countries, it has the potential to be one of the most dominant economies in the world by 2050.

Economic reform in the 1990s brought stability to the country's finances, putting behind it a history of boom and bust where high inflation and foreign debt hampered its development. Today, Brazil is the world's 7th largest economy and by far the largest in South America, representing over 50 per cent of regional GDP.

The UK enjoys a strong and historic trading relationship with Brazil, stretching back over 200 years. Today, Brazil remains the UK's most important trading partner in Latin America, with bilateral trade almost reaching £5 billion in 2010. The UK is also one of the largest investors in Brazil. However, there is strong evidence to suggest that many UK companies are not aware of the size and level of opportunity that exists in Brazil.

Chapter 2: Why Brazil?

Brazil is the world's seventh largest economy and by far the largest in South America.

Brazil is often described as a continent within a continent. São Paulo state alone is about the size of Great Britain. All of Western Europe would comfortably fit into Brazil with room to spare!

Brazil consists of 26 administrative states and the Federal District of Brasília, all with their own character, traditions and economic profiles. As a country of such magnitude and diversity, Brazil presents enormous potential for companies with persistence who are willing to invest time, money and effort. If you expect quick and easy results, you are likely to be disappointed.

Until comparatively recently, Brazil's broad industrial base supplied the domestic market. Although some of the larger multinationals such as GM, VW, Ericsson, Siemens and Fiat have been there for much longer, it was only at the beginning of the 1990s that Brazil's economy began to liberalise and open up to significant foreign industrial trade and investment. Brazil has been an agricultural exporter for much longer, but it is only recently that it has begun exporting large amounts of industrial and manufactured goods.

Today, Brazil is asserting its presence on the world stage as an emerging power and is enjoying its first sustained period of export-led growth in 20 years.

Consumers and businesses have developed higher standards, both for quality and value for money and Brazil has a large and prosperous middle class with an appetite for quality goods and services every bit as demanding as the consumer in London, Paris or New York. Against this background, Brazil has immense potential as a trade and investment partner, with huge opportunities for foreign companies across a range of sectors.

Doing business in Brazil can seem daunting for those new to the market, but taking a strategic approach is the key to making the process manageable. It is important to take a medium to long term view as success in Brazil requires commitment and patience. Brazil is one of the most promising and exciting major developing markets. However, it presents challenges in practical areas, such as communications, travel, product delivery and after sales service. If, after your initial background research, Brazil forms part of your strategic plan for overseas development, then you are ready to start the next phase will be market research.

In many sectors Brazil is already a well-developed market. You may find that your competitors are already there and that competition is fierce. As in any new market, you will need to use your competitive advantages to the full and it is important to know which ones will be the most effective in Brazil. You will need to research the market to identify the level of demand for your product and to decide whether you should address the market as a whole or via specific niches. Your initial research should tell you.

- Whether there is a market for your product in Brazil,
- If you should be targeting particular niches, and
- If you can be competitive in Brazil.

I'm thinking of doing business in Brazil but don't know where to begin!

Taking the strategic approach
- Leave your preconceptions at home.
- It is all too easy to be dazzled or overawed by Brazil, but keep hold of your business sense as tightly as you would anywhere.
- Do your homework on the market and on potential partners.
- Patience is a virtue. Some things may take longer to set up than you expect (especially if they involve bureaucracy), so allow for this in your preparations.
- Take a long-term approach, but do not always stick too rigidly to your plans. Things often change rapidly and unexpectedly in Brazil. Brazilians are flexible, and famous for finding a way around problems.
- Obtaining good-quality independent legal and professional advice is essential.
- If your product is in danger of being copied or counterfeited, seek specialist legal advice on how best to protect your intellectual property rights.
- Do not forget to carry out due diligence.

13

Once you have confirmed that there is a market for your product in Brazil, you may want to use the information you have gathered as a basis for developing a formal Brazil strategy.

This strategy should address questions such as the form of market entry (i.e. setting up a subsidiary, using a distributor or an agent, joint ventures, etc), identification of customers, potential partners, geographical locations, sales structure, product delivery, payment channels and after-sales set up.

Chapter 3: Market Entry Considerations

Legal advice

The importance of good quality independent legal advice, as in any foreign market, cannot be emphasised enough. It is essential to take this into consideration at the early stages of doing business in Brazil. Always seek good-quality independent legal advice before starting or signing anything that could have legal implications for your company, such as contracts or representation agreements. Specialist legal advice on intellectual property rights protection is also recommended and there are a number of highly qualified patent agents' firms available. Legal advice can be expensive, but it is money well spent.

It is far better to ensure that your interests in Brazil are fully protected than to leave yourself vulnerable to untoward consequences which can be even more expensive to sort out!

Once you have decided that entering the Brazilian market is right for your company, you will need to identify which part of the country you will start in unless, of course, you are doing business in Brazil as a result of an initial enquiry from a Brazilian company.

Brazil regional options; questions to ask yourself

- Where is there greatest demand for my product?
- Where is there greatest growth potential?
- How easy will it be to market, distribute and sell my product in the states I am looking at?
- What is the local/state authority's attitude to international trade?
- Do they welcome it or do they have a reputation for bureaucracy and obstructiveness?
- Who are my competitors?

São Paulo

The city of São Paulo is one of the largest metropolitan areas in the world and recognised as the business centre of Brazil. The interior of São Paulo state is also a very rich industrial and agricultural region, accounting for 25 per cent of the nation's industrial production.

Rio de Janeiro

Rio is the second-largest city in Brazil. Aside from tourism, Rio has a vibrant business district and is home to the dominant oil and gas industry, many of Brazil's largest companies and many multi-nationals.

Brasília

The economy of Brasília is driven by the federal government, which employs most of the city's workers. Aside from some light industry serving the needs of the city, there is little industry in Brasília.

Recife

Recife is one of the most important cities in the North East region, with a strong sense of a separate economic, political and cultural identity. Recife has a busy port and is the centre of aquaculture.

Porto Alegre

Porto Alegre, in the south of the country, considers itself the hub for Mercosul as it is only an hour's flight from all the major Mercosul business centres (São Paulo, Rio de Janeiro, Buenos Aires, Montevideo and Asunción).

Mercosul

Brazil is a huge market in its own right. However, it should also be viewed in the context of Mercosul (Mercosur in Spanish-speaking Latin America), the South American trading bloc that operates a similar principal of tariff-free trade to that of the EU between its member states. Mercosul encompasses Brazil, its largest and most influential member and neighbours Argentina, Uruguay, Paraguay and Venezuela. So in addition to the 185 million people in Brazil, there is a regional market of over 250 million!

You can find out more information by visiting: www.mercosur.int

Chapter 4: Agents and Distributors

To export successfully to Brazil you will probably need to employ an agent or distributor. An agent is a company's direct representative in a market and is paid commission, while a distributor sells products on to customers after buying them from the manufacturer; their income comes from the margin they can make on resale.

The Brazilian legal concept of a sales agent is rather broad, including almost any independent agent who works as an intermediary in the sales of products or services. Given the size of the country, many companies employ sales representatives so that they can take best advantage of Brazil's vast market potential. As a result, a number of rules have been established regulating the activities of autonomous commercial representatives ("sales agents") and creating an extremely protective environment for sales representatives in Brazil.

Employing an agent or distributor can have several advantages and can greatly reduce the set-up costs and time taken to enter the market.

By employing an agent or distributor, you gain the experience of a seasoned local who will have expert local knowledge and contacts, and you will have someone on the ground to look after your interests.

However, there are some drawbacks to this approach. Employing a third party will raise the cost of your products in the market and you will also lose some control over sales and/or marketing.

Using a distributor may also increase the risk of your product being copied or counterfeited. Some of the larger agents and distributors may manage so many product lines that not enough attention is given to yours. Consequently, as sales develop, you may wish to open a representative office or some other form of permanent representation.

To manage agents and distributors properly you will need to identify the agent or distributor that is right for you. The information below provides a checklist of issues you should take into account when looking for a suitable agent or distributor.

Once you have chosen an agent or distributor you will want to ensure that your products receive a fair share (or more than a fair share) of the agent's attention. This can be achieved as follows:

- Visiting as regularly as possible at senior management level; this shows interest in, and commitment to, the agent and the market. This will also provide you with an opportunity to learn about conditions in the market and see how your products are faring. This is particularly important in Brazil, where it is beneficial to develop personal relationships to do business. Distributors in Brazil often complain that their suppliers rarely visit the market. This can be one of the reasons why foreign suppliers fail to achieve their full market potential in Brazil.

- Working closely with your agents and distributors to show them how they can profit from your products.
- Helping to prepare marketing and sales plans for the agent.
- Providing regular training for the sales staff, and after sales training for the technical staff.
- Linking performance to incentives and agreeing milestone targets.

Finding the right agent or distributor

The checklist below details things you should bear in mind when looking for a suitable agent or distributor.

- Background
- Size of agency
- History of agency
- Other companies they act for
- What is the core business of the agent or distributor?
- Does the agent or distributor carry products that will compete with yours?
- Does the agent or distributor have qualified staff who can offer the necessary technical support, without which clients will not buy the products?
- Experience
- Number of sales people, their length of service and qualifications
- Success record

- Banking and trade references
- Distribution
- Geographical coverage
- Types of outlets covered
- Transportation
- Warehousing
- Are they right for your product?
- Knowledge of local market conditions
- Marketing competence
- Degree of English-language skills throughout the organisation
- Their interest in and enthusiasm for new products and yours in particular
- After-sales service levels
- Required skills of salespeople
- Personal relationships; this is very important in Brazil.

Chapter 5: Other Forms of Market Entry Strategies

As a rule, foreign firms who choose to set up a Brazilian company can establish either as a limited liability company (the most common corporate entity) or as a corporation. A Brazilian company is legally defined as one which is incorporated according to Brazilian law and has its head office in Brazil.

Corporations

The registered capital of corporations is divided into shares. Corporations can be capitalised either by private or public subscription. Open capital corporations offer public subscriptions by offering their shares to the public through the stock market. Closed capital corporations offer theirs privately to existing shareholders. If you are considering setting up or forming a company in Brazil, it is recommended that proper legal advice is sought.

If you decide to establish a permanent presence in Brazil, then the following steps are essential:

- Carry out thorough research and due diligence checks.
- Seek good-quality independent legal and professional advice.
- Allocate sufficient time and money to do this properly,
- Research local market conditions.

- Investigate any restrictions that may apply to your investment.
- Acquaint yourself with the relevant legal requirements and regulations.
- Identify the potential risks and plan for them, and get to grips with anything that might impact on your investment.

Direct and indirect investment

There are both direct and indirect investment options in Brazil. Direct investments are those made through a newly created corporate entity or by acquiring equity participation in existing Brazilian companies. Equity participation includes:

- Currency investments,
- Investment by conversion of foreign credits, and
- Investment by importation of goods without exchange cover.

Indirect investments are those made by foreign investors in the financial and securities markets where there is no requirement to establish or acquire participation in a Brazilian company.

Foreign branches

To set up a branch in Brazil a foreign company must submit an application to the Brazilian government, which must be approved by a Presidential decree.

A certificate of the decree will then be published in the Official Gazette, and a copy registered at the appropriate commercial registry. The branch can only start its activities when all the formalities have been completed. The foreign company must also empower a representative (who need not be Brazilian, but must be resident in Brazil) to act on its behalf.

Due to these complex and time-consuming requirements, you will probably only want to set up foreign branches in Brazil if this is required by law (e.g. for financial institutions and insurance companies).

Joint Venture

In Brazil, a joint venture is as the name suggests; an organisation jointly owned by a Brazilian and a foreign partner, and was for a long time the only option available for foreign investment in Brazil. In some sectors, a joint venture is still the only permitted route for establishing a permanent presence.

Joining forces with a Brazilian partner can be beneficial if you wish to sell direct to the Brazilian domestic market. You will be able to take advantage of the Brazilian partner's contacts and local knowledge, while they in turn benefit from technology transfer or your company's expertise in other areas. However, the major concern with joint ventures is finding a partner with whom you can work. Many joint ventures fail where, for example, due regard has not been given to the importance which Brazilians attach to personal relationships in business. It is often better to select a joint venture partner who complements you rather than a potential competitor.

Plan for your exit from a joint venture from the outset; it is rare that joint ventures are permanent, and it is better to have a "pre-nuptial agreement" than a messy divorce. If you do decide to go down this route, it is essential that you carry out thorough due diligence checks on your potential partner.
While no specific Brazilian law governs joint ventures, they are usually classified under two types; contractual joint ventures and corporate joint ventures.

Under a contractual joint venture, it is not necessary to set up a Brazilian company. This type of joint venture is a co-operation mechanism between the parties whereby the profit or loss distribution, and the relative management, can be freely stipulated.

Under a corporate joint venture, a Brazilian company will be incorporated under the limited liability or corporation format. Although there is no specific law in Brazil relating to joint ventures, the laws on mergers and acquisitions should be taken into account when establishing a corporate joint venture.

Chapter 6: Due Diligence

In order to create a favourable impression of your company and your product in Brazil, it is essential to have a name that Brazilian consumers can remember. If a product name cannot be remembered, it is unlikely that many people will buy it. It is not advisable to have a Portuguese translation of your company name. English names are very well accepted by Brazilians.

However, it is advisable to spend some time on getting this right. The name is, after all, the first thing your potential customers will see.

Due diligence is a security measure that companies often choose to undertake in order to check the viability of potential new business before contracts are signed.

Due diligence is strongly advisable, particularly in connection with the acquisition of a shareholding interest either in a limited liability company or a corporation, and in the acquisition of all quotas of a limited liability company or shares of a corporation.

For practical purposes, it is recommended that due diligence covers all accounting, tax and legal issues concerning a particular business enterprise. Special attention should be given to ongoing, or threatened, commercial and tax claims at administrative and judicial level.

Wherever the purchase of property is involved, a review of the Real Estate Registry status is crucial to establish that the seller has the valid title, and that the property is free and unencumbered.

Branding Due diligence

The language spoken in Brazil is Brazilian Portuguese. The differences between Brazilian and European Portuguese are slight and are similar to those between British and American English (i.e. differing accents and some different words). Making the effort demonstrates seriousness about entering the Brazilian market and any attempt to communicate in Portuguese will be met with a positive response.

Where a visitor possesses no Portuguese language skills, Spanish or Italian can be useful to communicate basic messages, and Brazilians will find it fairly easy to understand "Portuñol", the mixture of Spanish and Portuguese spoken by many Spanish-speaking Latin American visitors to Brazil. However, do not assume that Spanish will always be welcome. The best advice is to offer a "disclaimer" i.e. "I'm sorry I don't speak much Portuguese, but I do speak English and some Spanish". If you start speaking Spanish directly, Brazilians might think that you don't know that their first language is Portuguese and it will give a bad impression.

While an increasing number of Brazilian companies, particularly those with an international outlook, have English speakers on their staff, do not assume that everyone speaks English. It is advisable to engage a local interpreter to accompany you to your first meeting with a potential partner until you have established whether your partner is confident doing business in English. Your interpreter will be one of your key assets and should be selected with care.

Initial written approaches to Brazilian companies should always be in Brazilian Portuguese and company literature (including a basic company profile and product descriptions/ profiles) should also be translated into Portuguese. It is courteous to have your business card translated into Portuguese too.

Chapter 7: Culture and Communication

It still surprises me to hear some people say that "anything below Mexico is all the same." Well, let me just say that this is as far from the truth as you can get. For starters, in Brazil they speak Portuguese and not Spanish. And yes, Spanish and Portuguese speakers can understand each other to a certain extent but if you plan on being successful in Brazil, you definitely need to learn Portuguese. You need to know at least enough that people see you are trying. If you get there speaking Spanish, people may not be as warm as you probably hear they are. When it comes to business then things can get really interesting. And I don't say this in a positive way.

In a country that has about 200 million people, one cannot expect that everyone will be the same. Brazil is the 5th largest country in the world and one of the most diverse places in the globe. Depending on the region you will find influences from Africa, Holland, France, Germany, Poland, Italy, Japan and many others. Brazil is a true melting pot so if you plan on being successful there it's imperative that you do your homework on the region you are going to be investing in.

A lot of businesses don't think of cultural and language training as an investment and I am here to argue the opposite. I was just in Brazil and I met with a lot of influential people. A lot of them told me stories of businesses going bad because people didn't know how to talk, how to respect their space, and their country. Don't think for a second that the "one size fits all" approach works for every market. Know that Brazil is one of these unique places where you not only have to adapt to the country but also to a specific region. If you are investing in a product or service in Bahia, it may not be as suitable to Rio Grande do Sul and vice versa.

Now that Brazil is in the spotlight, this is the time for you to do things right. You have only one chance so do it right the first time. Learn the language, spend time in the country, talk to the people, participate in cultural events, be flexible and work with people who can understand your culture as well as Brazil's. You will be glad you did!

It is essential that you request Brazilian Portuguese translation of your literature. A very common mistake is to request a translation into Portuguese without stressing that it should be Brazilian Portuguese. The resulting literature will be seen by Brazilian businesses as demonstrating both a lack of knowledge of the country and a degree of rudeness.

Language

- Brazilians communicate with a blunt cultural style. However, this is often determined by the level of a relationship i.e. the warmer it is, the blunter it gets.
- Brazilians place a lot of emphasis on non-verbal gestures to enhance their point.

- Communication is generally very polite. However Brazilians' conversations can be held at breakneck speed, with plenty of animation, frequent interruptions and lots of physical contact.
- Brazilians like depth, background and context. You should consider offering more information than you normally would.

If Brazil is likely to become a significant part of your business, you should consider hiring a Portuguese-speaking member of staff. You may also wish to take up the challenge of learning Portuguese yourself even having a basic level of communication will create a positive impression and will have the added benefit of making your trips to Brazil more enjoyable. However, even if you do attain a reasonable level of fluency, an interpreter or a Portuguese speaking member of staff will be essential in business meetings.

Day-to-day communications

Once you have made contact with a Brazilian company, it is likely that your day-to-day telephone and email communications will be in English with one of their English-speaking members of staff. If you do not think the standard of English in the Brazilian company is up to scratch, you might wish to ask for parallel Portuguese texts and get them translated; this could be a valuable investment. An important part of setting up arrangements in Brazil is to ensure that communication issues are covered in detail. Most failures occur in business relationships because of fractured communications and mutual misunderstandings.

In any case, both parties should agree in writing the language of official documents. This is to avoid endless disputes about meaning and definition between two versions of the same contract. In the event of a dispute, a judge will want to know whether the English or the Portuguese version is the official one.

Chapter 8: Intellectual Property Rights and Documentation

In principle, Brazil has a sound intellectual property rights and patent system that does not discriminate unduly against foreign companies. However, the effectiveness and impartiality of enforcement is variable and any legal processes will be both protracted and costly.

A new Trademark and Patent agreement law was enacted in Brazil in 1996 which follows international standards and general guidelines established by TRIPS (the Trade-Related Aspects of Intellectual Property Rights). This has encouraged substantial investment in the country, both in the construction of new manufacturing facilities and in research and development in the pharmaceutical and biotechnology industries.

For companies whose business involves intellectual property, there are issues of piracy to consider, particularly for goods such as books, CDs, textiles, cosmetics and spare parts. While the Brazilian Government has made some progress on intellectual property rights legislation and implementation, there is scope for further progress.

Brazil is a signatory to the main intellectual property treaties and is a member of the World Intellectual Property Organisation. Its legal provisions are therefore generally consistent with international standards.

It is very important that you comply with all aspects of Brazilian regulations on documentation. The necessity of this cannot be overemphasised as this is a source of frequent difficulties between supplier and buyer. A good partner and/or freight forwarder with a local office in Brazil can provide invaluable advice on documentation.

A commercial invoice and bill of lading/air waybill are required, as are sanitary certificates for the shipment of certain goods. These documents must show the import licence number issued by SECEX (the Brazilian Foreign Trade Secretariat). The commercial invoice should be completed by the supplier in the country of origin and show full details of the goods.

The general documentation requirements for Brazil are:
- Customs Import Declaration
- Simplified Import Declaration
- Declaration of Customs Value
- Import Licence
- Commercial Invoice
- Pro Forma Invoice
- Air Waybill
- Bill of Lading
- Certificate of Origin
- Packing List

Some goods may be subject to additional documentation, such as sanitary certificates, licences, permits and certificates of free sale.

Import Certificates

The number and date of issue of the import certificate must be shown on the commercial invoice immediately following the declaration of the merchandise (i.e. the description and value of the consignment).

Certificates of Origin

Satisfactory proof of origin of the merchandise must be provided by the exporter to the importer for submission to Brazilian customs. Usually the original plus four copies of the invoices are given to the British or Brazilian Chamber of Commerce for certification. The original plus three copies appropriately certified will then be returned to the exporter.

SITTER-aligned documentation is available for Brazil. SITTER is a special certified invoice overlay which enables the required declaration to be produced electronically on a computer screen template, on the lower quarter of the export invoice (ref 380-1).

Certificates of Free Sale

A Certificate of Free Sale can be required to show that goods are available for retail sale, that they comply with EU regulations and are suitable for use by EU consumers.

Second-hand goods

Applications for import licences for second-hand goods must be accompanied by a technical report issued by SGS United Kingdom Ltd, (www.uk.sgs.com) or another such company appointed by the Brazilian Embassy in London, evaluating the condition of the equipment. The import will also have to meet further criteria determined by the individual nature of the consignment.

Export Licences

Export controls apply to goods upon which the UK Government has placed export licensing requirements. Typically, export controls relate to goods that may be used in some way for military applications, goods of national heritage (e.g. works of art), and certain chemicals used in the production of controlled drugs.

Export documentation

SITPRO is the UK's trade facilitation body dedicated to encouraging and helping businesses to trade more effectively, and to simplifying the international trading process. It focuses on the procedures and documentation associated with international trade. SITPRO offers advice on the documents and procedures for the movement of goods through its briefings, completion guides and checklists

Duties and taxes

It is important to know what import duties a product will attract when it lands in Brazil. High duties may make an export too expensive for the Brazilian market.

In addition to import duties, taxes such as COF (the Social Security tax), STT (the State Tax of 17 or 18 per cent), PIS, ICMS (VAT) and IPI are levied against products' duty-paid value. We recommend the European Commission's Market Access Database as a useful resource to research how much it will cost to import your product: http://mkaccdb.eu.int/

The Market Access Database is a free tool designed to assist exporters:
- It provides information on trade barriers which may affect you in overseas markets.
- The Applied Tariff Database section allows users to enter a Harmonised System code or product description to obtain a tariff rate and details of taxes applicable, enabling you to calculate a landed cost.
- The Exporters' Guide to Import Formalities database (searchable by Harmonised System code or by product), gives an overview of import procedures and documents, as well as any general and specific requirements for a product.

- The Sanitary and Phytosanitary Database facilitates the identification of sanitary and phytosanitary export problems with any non-EU country.

The Market Access Database can only be accessed through an internet service provider that is based in the EU.

Tariff Harmonised System Code

The Harmonised System (HS) code is an international method of classifying products for export purposes. This classification is used by customs officials around the world to determine the duties, taxes and regulations that apply to the product.

Although it is advisable to insert the details of the HS code of the product to be exported to Brazil on the Invoice and Certificate of Origin where required, only the first four digits of the HS code should be inserted, as these are common for every country in the world under the HS rule.

The importer must consult the Brazilian import tariff for the rest of the tariff code number to satisfy the Brazilian customs authorities at the time of import of the consignment. The full tariff code required by the Brazilian customs authority may differ significantly from that ascertained by the exporter from the Market Access Database. Although the Market Access Database can be used for reference purposes, it is the prime responsibility of the importer to make their own import declaration to customs, and thus use their own national tariff for this purpose.

Commercial samples and temporary imports

Regulations governing the import of samples are complicated, and samples should not be sent to Brazil except by prior arrangement. Some samples may require previous authorisation from specific government departments in Brazil, such as the Ministry of Health and the Ministry of Agriculture. Samples cannot be sent if the product is forbidden. Commercial travellers can import small quantities of samples of no commercial value in their baggage without payment of duty. You may take in samples of value on a duty-free basis subject to the posting of a bond to Brazilian customs at the point of entry into the country, to cover payment of any duties and taxes payable if the samples are not re-exported. Samples imported under these arrangements must be listed. Two copies of the list, signed by the traveller's company, are required to be kept by the traveller when they arrive in Brazil, for submission to customs at the point of arrival if required. If the samples are to be distributed to potential customers, proper records should be kept concerning how many samples and their value were given away. All other items retained by the traveller should be noted and recorded for the purposes of exit from the country.

Chapter 9: Labelling and Packaging Legislation

Brazil now has very strict legislation for the import of certain products, especially in the food and health sectors. Some products need to be registered with the Health Inspection Agency before they are allowed to enter the country, and this process can be expensive, complicated and time consuming.

Labelling and packaging

Imported products can be sold in Brazil in their original packaging provided a label is attached, giving the following information in Brazilian Portuguese:

- A description of the product.
- The weight (metric) according to local standards.
- The composition of the product.
- Its validity (sell-by date or expiry)
- The country of origin.
- The name and address of the importer, and any special warning on risks to health or security.

Usually this label is placed on the product in Brazil by the importer. Special labelling regulations apply to imported pharmaceutical specialities, antiseptics, disinfectants, cosmetics, beauty and hygienic preparations, alcoholic beverages and foodstuffs.

The Brazilian government requires the pre-approval of all animal product labels. This is usually the responsibility of the exporter, through his agent or representative, or importer. For a foreign company to become an approved supplier of foodstuffs, in Brazil their local importer has to prepare a Brazilian Portuguese translation of the company's labelling and submit it, along with the required questionnaire, to the Brazilian Department of Animal Origin Products (DIPOA).

The foreign company will need to supply the following information.

- Name of the product.
- Ingredients and country of origin.
- Special storage instructions (where necessary).
- Net weight (in metric units).
- Date of production (must be identified on master carton).
- Expiration date (shelf life, established by the manufacturer).

When an instruction manual accompanies any specific product it must also be in Brazilian Portuguese.

Certificate of Quality

All products imported into Brazil also require a Certificate of Quality, which must be supplied in order for the Brazilian importer to obtain the necessary import licence. Foreign manufactured goods will require certificates issued by the ISO (International Standards Organisation)

Foreign-made goods will require certificates supplied by the appropriate standards organisation in the original country of manufacture. The Brazilian Standards Organisation is INMETRO National Institute of Metrology, Standardization and Industrial Quality – www.inmetro.gov.br.

Details of shipment

For the purposes of import clearance, all invoices, packing lists and shipping documents should contain the clearest information possible concerning the consignment being shipped, with specific details of the description of the goods and quantities thereof. Under the new World Customs Organisation freight security initiatives, the phrases "Said to Contain" and "Freight of all Kinds" are no longer acceptable and must be avoided.

It is also wise to plan ahead when making marine shipments to Brazil. Journey times can be several weeks, and there are not many shipping lines making direct sailings to Brazil. Check details of sailings through your local freight forwarder or through Lloyd's Loading List, as well as obtaining competitive quotes for freight rates. Remember, the higher the freight cost, the more import duty the Brazilian importer will have to pay. The Import Landed Cost comprises Cost, Insurance and Freight (CIF).

Chapter 10: Getting Paid

The Brazilian currency is the Real, and it is quoted on all the main foreign exchange markets. Check each day on the exchange rate on internet. There is also a branch of Brazil's main bank, the Banco do Brasil, in the City of London and all major capital cities in the world, and they can assist with foreign exchange matters where required. Transactions with Brazil can also be negotiated in US dollars.

Short-term finance

When exporting to Brazil normal commercial rules should be followed. You should discuss the arrangements for security of payment with the international department of your bank, the offices of Brazilian banks in your country or banks based in your country who have offices in Brazil.

If you are a first-time exporter to Brazil, the standard method of receiving payment for your goods is by documentary Letter of Credit. The opening of the documentary Letter of Credit is based on the contract signed between the Brazilian buyer and the foreign seller. There are no problems regarding Letters of Credit opened by Brazilian banks being accepted by foreign banks. The Brazilian bank will make payment provided that the requirements of the Letter of Credit are met.

However, you should be aware that a Letter of Credit is a form of contract between two banks. A bank will make payment provided that the documents submitted to it are in strict compliance with the conditions of the Letter of Credit. This is regardless of the purchase contract. To prevent the possibility of a payment being made if the terms of the purchase contract are not met, the seller should check the Letter of Credit against the terms of the purchase contract and request amendments from the buyer if necessary.

Open Account and Bills for Collection are other payment methods commonly used between foreign exporters and Brazilian importers when a trustworthy relationship between the two parties has been developed. Major exports and those requiring long-term finance will require specialist payment and financing.

It can be beneficial for foreign companies to offer financial support (i.e. credit) to importers of capital goods into Brazil. Such support is often offered as part of a deal by German or US suppliers which they have put together with support from banks in their own countries, with interest rates far below those available from banks in Brazil. Brazilian interest rates are generally significantly higher than those in the EU. This access to favourable payment terms can make a critical difference in negotiations between foreign suppliers and Brazilian importers.

The Brazilian currency is not freely negotiable and foreign currency can only be purchased for transactions that are authorised and controlled by the Central Bank. The appropriate documentary evidence must be presented to authorised brokers for the purchase of foreign currency. Since January 1999, the Brazilian currency has been allowed to float. There are no restrictions on the remittance of profits.

Chapter 11: Contracts, Pricing and Insurance

Brazilians usually have the same approach as Europeans, using a standard contract and altering it to fit different circumstances, and signing the revised version would seem straightforward. However, this will again depend on the organisation, size of the company and type of business involved. For some, to start a business relationship with a contract might be seen as overly formal, as for them a balanced relationship should begin based on trust, leaving lawyers to one side, at least until a later stage.

Brazilian importers tend to use a standard form of contract in their transactions. Foreign contracts are seldom accepted for fear of being trapped by unfamiliar contract stipulations. Adding special provisions to the standard contract form is normally acceptable.

Dispute resolution

For a contract or a copy of a document to be automatically recognised in court it usually has to be notarised. It is strongly recommended that you avoid having Brazilian courts decide any disputes between parties, as they can be slow and unfamiliar with cross border disputes. A good alternative now available under Brazilian law is the use of arbitration, which allows the parties to choose any person or chamber (such as the International Chamber of Commerce or the London Court of International Arbitration) to arbitrate disputes.

Pricing

Pricing should be competitive and can usually be negotiated in US dollars or Brazilian Reais. Brazilian Portuguese should be used if possible and all costs should be included.

Brazilian exporters usually conduct transactions at Free On Board prices, whereas importers would search to find the most cost-effective alternative.

Insurance

Commercial insurance in Brazil usually covers transportation insurance, financial insurance, fire insurance and multi-risk insurance.

The private sector provides credit insurance for exports of consumer goods, raw materials and other similar goods. Speak to your banker or insurance broker for more information.

Private sector insurance has some limitations though, particularly for sales of capital goods, major services and construction projects that require longer credit packages or are in riskier markets.

Bribery and corruption

There can be problems with bribery and corruption in Brazil. If you believe what you see in the media, it pervades all sections of society from the residents of shanty towns paying for protection, to business people wanting to get their goods into the country more quickly, to politicians who appear keen to make money from jumping allegiances at the drop of a hat. In 2010, Transparency International's Corruption Perceptions Index rated Brazil in 69th place out of 178 countries but above fellow BRIC markets China, India and Russia. The Brazilian Government appears to be making some moves in the right direction, but many view these as insufficient to engender real change.

However, most international companies operating in Brazil and most of the large Brazilian companies and organisations now frown on any illegal practices. The majority of business deals are corruption free and, while you should be aware of the possibility of illegal practices, you should not indulge in the hope of getting business quickly.

Chapter 12: Meeting and Business Etiquette

Before conducting business in Brazil, you should be aware of the local customs that need to be taken into account. Brazil's business culture is largely southern European, with considerable influence from Africa and Asia regionally. In commercial hubs such as São Paulo you will find a sophisticated and developed commercial environment.

In São Paulo and the south of Brazil there is a strong influence from the descendants of Italians and the Portuguese, Spanish and Japanese. Rio de Janeiro has a more laid-back feel and the further north you go the greater the difference to the atmosphere in the south of Brazil. Establishing personal relationships is essential to conducting business throughout the country.

Greeting etiquette

First names should normally be used, but titles are important. When meeting and greeting expect a firm handshake, often for a long time, combined with strong eye contact. Both men and women greet women with a kiss on each cheek.

On departure you should repeat all the handshaking and kissing and it can take 10 minutes to get out of a room! Time should be included in your programme;

don't assume that you will be able to make a quick exit.

Meeting etiquette

Conservative European dress code is the norm for all meetings in big cities such as São Paulo and Rio de Janeiro. In the tropical north and north east of Brazil, where temperatures can reach 40°C, smart casual dress may be acceptable, or even desirable, if visiting external sites, but, if in doubt, you should ask beforehand.

When arranging a meeting, it is advisable to provide the Brazilian company with the subject of the meeting in advance, although only limited detail will be required at that stage.

Punctuality can sometimes be an issue in Brazil, but you should not interpret lateness as a sign of rudeness or laziness. If you will be late for a business meeting, you should call the Brazilian company to advise them. However, be aware that the Brazilians will be making jokes among themselves about the British always being punctual! Traffic in Brazil, especially in big cities like São Paulo and Rio de Janeiro, can be bad. Plan your trip with plenty of time to allow for delays.

Meetings can be lengthy affairs, allowing for small talk before getting down to business. It is normal to exchange business cards at the start of meetings (although in restaurants or at business lunches they should be exchanged after the meal). It is polite to turn off your mobile (or leave it mute) during meetings and business lunches or dinners, only taking urgent calls. If you are expecting an urgent call, it is wise to inform your contact in advance.

You should not expect to do any business around Carnival week (which immediately precedes Lent, seven weeks ahead of Easter). Indeed, as Carnival usually falls in February, this is not a month in which you should travel to Brazil with the intention of doing business. The same is true for the Christmas and New Year period and, to a lesser extent, the July school holidays.

Entertainment

Food is big in Brazil, in both its importance socially and the portions served. Formal lunches and dinners have always been a part of doing business in Brazil. Sometimes it is easier to invite a senior contact for a meal than for a meeting at the company.

Lunches and dinners are seen as an opportunity to socialise and to get to know each other in more depth and Brazilians enjoy taking this time. These are also seen as good opportunities to do business. In Brazil, there is no "grab-a-sandwich" culture.

Frequent toasts to good health are standard. You can drink alcoholic or non-alcoholic drinks for toasts. If you host a meal, soft drinks and juices should be available.

Brazilians do not arrive on time for social functions; they usually arrive 15 minutes after the agreed time. After a meal is finished they usually stay to socialise.

Lunch in Brazil is served from 12.30 to 14.30 and dinner from about 20.30 to 22.30.

In general, Brazilians tend to be very flexible and adaptable and use common sense. Due to decades of economic instability, hyperinflation and awkward government policies that influenced life and business, the Brazilian businessperson has become short-term minded, with a great ability to review plans, and improvise. Improvisation has a strong presence in people's habits and business in general.

Although Brazilians are concerned with quality, price is usually the key factor to determine the success of a business partnership. Brazilians tend to avoid exclusive agreements and being dependent on a single supplier. They can also be extremely careful if there are doubts or uncertainties, and a deal can take months before a final agreement is reached. In Brazil, the understanding and concept of timing depends on many factors, including with whom and where business is being conducted. It is important to get to know as much as possible about your potential business partner this can give you an indication as to how he/she deals with timing and deadlines.

When dealing with the public sector things can be very different. Brazil has a high level of bureaucracy and a very intricate legal system, and any deals or processes can be conducted at a very slow pace. In these cases, local expertise is necessary and always welcome.

- Expect a great deal of time to be spent reviewing details. Often the people you negotiate with will not have decision-making authority.
- Use local lawyers and accountants for negotiations.
- Brazilians resent an outside legal presence.
- Brazilian business is hierarchical. Decisions are made by the highest ranking person.
- Brazilians negotiate with people, not companies. Do not change your negotiating team or you may have to start over again from the beginning.

If you choose to do business in Brazil, try to learn a little about the country first. Brazil is vast and diverse. Many cultures from Europe, Asia, Africa and the Middle East have contributed to form the nation. Brazil hosts some of the world's largest immigrant populations of Lebanese, Japanese, Germans, Italians and Portuguese, and large African and Jewish communities, as well as many other minorities, such as Polish, Hungarians, Palestinians, native Indians and many others. These groups have generally intermarried and mixed their cultures under the same language and general understanding of nationality. In some areas of the country, however, a dominant influence of one original culture can still be evident. This naturally creates variations in the behaviours of the people with regard to relationships, business and the way of life.

This melting pot of different cultures makes it difficult to define a standard behaviour throughout the country or to establish a general cultural trait that defines a Brazilian.

Sophisticated presentations with multiple illustrations are the norm for many forward-looking Brazilian companies, and it is advisable to take the same approach to create a good impression. Handouts and brochures in Brazilian Portuguese are recommended.

Never start a presentation apologetically. During presentations avoid slang and jokes specific to your culture and geography. Your Brazilian audience may not understand. There is no need to be extremely formal. Do not speak too quickly, loudly, or in a monotonous tone.

At the beginning of the presentation make it clear to the audience whether you prefer to take questions during or after the talk. Often, audiences are happier writing down their questions rather than asking them in front of others.

If there is not enough time to take all written questions, tell the audience that you will reply to them by email and do so.

A good interpreter is the key to successful communication. If your audience has not understood what you have said, your message will be lost on them.

A growing number of Brazilian executives and government officials speak some English. However, on setting up an appointment, you should always ask if your contact speaks English or would feel more comfortable with an interpreter.

There are two forms of interpreting. Consecutive interpreting means you speak and then your interpreter interprets; this is the usual form for meetings, discussions and negotiations. Simultaneous interpreting is when you speak while the interpreter interprets simultaneously; but special equipment is required which is expensive to hire. Simultaneous interpreting is generally used only for large seminars and conferences.

Interpreting is a skill requiring professional training. Just because someone is fluent in English and Portuguese it does not mean that they will make a good interpreter.

If you are giving a speech or presentation, remember that the need to interpret everything will cut your available speaking time approximately in half (unless using simultaneous interpreting). It is essential to make sure that the interpreter can cope with any technical or specialist terms in the presentation. It is better to be slightly restricted and speak close to a script than to fail to be understood because your interpreter cannot follow you. If you are giving a speech, give the interpreter the text well in advance and forewarn them of any changes.

Below are a number of recommendations for getting the best out of your interpreter:

- Though expensive, a well-briefed professional interpreter is best.

- Try to involve your interpreter at every stage of your pre-meeting arrangements. The quality of interpretation will improve greatly if you provide adequate briefing on the subject matter. Ensure your interpreter understands what you are aiming to achieve.

- Speak clearly and evenly, without rambling on for several paragraphs without pause. Your interpreter will find it hard to remember everything you have said, let alone interpret all your points if you speak at length.

- Conversely, do not speak in short phrases and unfinished sentences. Your interpreter may find it impossible to translate the meaning if you have left a sentence hanging.

- Avoid jargon, unless you know your interpreter is familiar with the terminology.

- Take into account that some interpreters may be more familiar with American English and have a little difficulty at first with British accents.

- Listen to how your interpreter interprets what you have just said. If you have given a lengthy explanation but the interpreter translates into only a few Portuguese words, it may be that they have not fully understood. Or they may be wary of passing on a message that is too blunt and will not be well received by the audience.

- Avoid jokes. They will fall flat, embarrass you, and leave the audience puzzled. And remember: in Brazil, the official language is Portuguese, not "Brazilian"!

Building relationships

Relationships in Brazil are important, but again this can vary between regions and backgrounds. For some businesspeople, it is vital to develop a strong relationship to allow business to flow better. For others, it is not so important. In general, it is usually more productive to start by creating a relaxed, transparent and friendly atmosphere.

An overly professional and direct way of negotiating for the European business person would not usually go down well with most Brazilians. Stiff and aggressive negotiating attitudes generally do not help to bring about the best results.

Learning Portuguese is obviously of benefit. If you don't have time to become conversant, making the effort to learn basic pleasantries can go down well. The differences between Brazilian and European Portuguese are similar to those between British and American English (i.e. with differing accents and some different words). Any attempt to speak a little will be well received, even if incorrect.

Brazilians tend to speak quite loudly, especially in casual situations. This can appear strange at first to the foreign ear. Long, animated conversation is a favourite Brazilian habit. When conversing, interruptions are viewed as enthusiasm. Brazilians enjoy joking, informality, and friendships.

- Good conversation topics include football, family, children and music.
- Bad conversation topics include Argentina, politics, poverty, religion and the rainforest. Don't worry too much about this though as Brazilians are gracious, forgiving and not easily offended.

If this is your first visit to Brazil, you should expect to be asked if you like it. Brazilians are universally keen to know that visitors have a positive impression of their country, as they are intensely patriotic.

Body language
- Brazilians speak in very close proximity, with lots of physical contact.
- Touching arms and elbows is the norm.
- Back slapping is very common between men.
- Eye contact is expected.
- The 'OK' hand signal is a rude gesture in Brazil.

Brazilians will want to reinforce their business relationship with you by visiting your country, once a deal has been or is likely to be done, so be sure to invite them at the end of your first meeting if appropriate. Indeed, they will probably be delighted to visit your country, especially if it is for the first time.

Chapter 13: Overseas Business Risk Brazil

Information on key security and political risks which foreign businesses may face when operating in Brazil.

Political and Economic

The Federal Republic of Brazil is divided into twenty six states and one federal district. The legislative branch is made of a bicameral National Congress which consists of the Federal Senate and the Chamber of Deputies. As a democratic country Brazil holds elections for four-year terms by popular vote. The suffrage is compulsory between 18 and 70 years of age, and voluntary between 16 and 18 and over 70.

Since 1st January 2011, as result of the victory of the Workers' Party (Partido dos Trabalhadores- PT) in the previous year, Brazil has as President Dilma Rousseff, the first woman in the country's history in this position. The party also has majority of seats in the Chamber of Deputies.

Some R\$4.6bn worth of amendments to the 2009 budget, mostly for local public works projects, was due to expire at the end of this month but Dilma extended the deadline for the release of these funds by three months after congressional leaders had threatened a major rebellion.

President Dilma launched a new social programme to eradicate extreme poverty, 'Brasil sem Miséria' (Brazil without Misery). The programme aims to lift the remaining 16 million Brazilians out of extreme poverty during the next four years. Tackling poverty was a key element of Dilma's election campaign and is her top priority for government.

As expected, Brazil eventually backed Christine Lagarde as the next IMF head, going against its Latin American neighbours. Brazil supported Lagarde's pro-reform platform, in an attempt to increase the voices of small economies.

Brazil remains embroiled in trade disputes, such as the standoff with Argentina. The requirement for non-automatic import licenses remains, though issuance will be sped up to within the 60-day period mandated by the WTO. Although this measure was applied for all countries, there is no evidence that it is affecting UK products.

Economic Overview

In the last decade Brazil has shown economic stability and was one of the first countries to recover from the crisis of 2008/2009 with a GDP growth of 7.5% in 2010 (about £ 1,300 billion). The country is a member of Mercosul, and is the biggest economy in South America, accounting for over 50% of the continent's GDP. The attractiveness to foreign investors is justified by its solid economic fundamentals (with Brazil holding an Investment Grade from all three main ratings agencies) and its large consumer market.

Unemployment rate reached its lowest level since 2002, 6% and the government expects to create more 2.7 million new positions, totalling 5.5 million in 2012. Many of these 'new positions' represent a formalization of jobs from the informal economy, which remains significant.

New data revealed that more than 35 million Brazilians moved from classes D and E to class C between 2002 and 2010. In recent years, Brazil is the only BRIC country that successfully achieved high economic growth rates while reducing inequalities. With a high propensity to consume, this new middle class represents a huge opportunity for companies to exploit which will be reinforced by the 13% minimum wage increase next year and a favourable demographic profile for the next 30 years.

Brazil has a diverse economy with a strong domestic services sector representing 67% of the GDP. Growth in this sector in the past year has been pushed by services of financial intermediation and insurances, and commerce. Industry and agriculture account for 26% and 6% of the Brazilian GDP, respectively. Brazil's main agricultural products are coffee, soybeans, wheat, rice, corn, sugarcane, cocoa, citrus and beef. Its main industry products are shoes, chemicals, textiles, lumber, iron ore, cement, tin, steel, aircraft, motor vehicles, machinery and equipment.

Regarding trade, Brazil remains a balanced but relatively closed economy. Brazilian exports reached US$ 201.9 billion in 2010, mostly made up of ores, oil and fuel, transport materials, soybeans, sugar and ethanol, chemicals and meat. In 2010, Brazil's main buyer was China with a 15.3% share of Brazil's exports, followed by U.S. with 9.6%, Argentina with 9.3%, Netherlands with 5.1%, and Germany with 4%.

Brazilian imports were US$ 181.6 billion in 2010, made up mainly of machinery, chemical products, oil, automotive parts, electrical and transport equipment and electronics. In 2010 15% of Brazilian imports came from the U.S., 14.1% from China, 7.9% from Argentina, 6.9% from Germany, and 4.6% from South Korea. Asia was in the first position of buyer for Brazilian products in 2010, surpassing Latin America and the European Union.

Bribery and Corruption

Brazil is among the world's leading investment destinations. However, despite a formally well-functioning business environment, corruption and bribery are still serious obstacles to doing business in Brazil. Especially in business dealings with the government at the local levels, corruption reportedly represents a serious threat.

Some positive developments in relation to corruption and investment can be recognised as Brazil is often cited for its strong legal framework expected to decreasing corruption, and the country is occasionally used as a role model for other developing countries, yet effective enforcement of laws is a problem.

Corruption is common in some environments, especially when it comes to speeding up bureaucratic processes. In 2010, Brazil was ranked 69 out of 178 in the Transparency International's corruption perception index (CPI).

There is a wide range of regulatory agencies due to the federal structure of the political system, which may increase the likelihood of demands for bribes by public officials.

Multiple corruption scandals have emerged over the years, involving politicians and bureaucrats taking kickbacks from companies in exchange for awarding public contracts.

The Brazilian tax system is complex and reportedly prone to corruption. It is reported that tax collectors frequently ask for bribes to relax assessments and inspections, to refrain from pursuing acts of tax fraud or to give advice on the legal possibilities of reducing tax obligations.

Entrepreneurs may find difficulties in navigating complex systems and vested interests when setting businesses up in Brazil. UK businesses should consider, in most cases, engaging a local partner when establishing interests in Brazil.

Local labour law is complex and onerous and requires careful handling to avoid incurring potentially expensive liabilities. There is a well-developed system of HR managers and lawyers that can offer expert advice on how best to manage employment. This is again another area where the right local partner could be essential for successful market entry.

Chapter 14: Opportunities During and Beyond 2012 World Cup and 2016 Olympics

Now we will take a look at other areas offering investment opportunities prior, during and beyond the 2014 World Cup and 2016 Olympics.

The purpose of this chapter is to come up with some investment opportunity areas related to the major sports events Brazil is hosting in the next few years. Even though the 2012 Brazilian GDP's first quarter growth wasn't what economists expected, (it just grew about 0.2%) a lot still needs to be done and invested for the country to organize well these events and take advantage of it all afterwards.

Last year a Brazilian institution called SEBRAE, which helps and advises mainly owners of small businesses, released a "map of opportunities" related to the sports events.

According to FGV (Fundacao Getulio Vargas) and Ernest&Young estimates, Brazil is expected to invest about R$22,46Bi (U$11Bi aprox) in infrastructure, R$309Mi (U$150Mi aprox) in IT, and R$6Bi (U$3Bi aprox) in services related to tourism. These estimates take into consideration mainly the 2010-2016 periods, including the pre-event and event phases, with the post-event phase (after 2016) being mainly the investment legacy these opportunities would have created and built.

The main sectors to receive investments are: construction, IT, Tourism (which includes productions associated with this sector), and services. Other sectors, probably not in a very large scale as the ones mentioned above, may also be favoured, such as agribusiness, sustainability, and sports marketing and events services.

The construction sector was broken down into another area, which includes administrative, supervision and management, raw materials supply, projects, and construction areas.

The administrative area includes everything related to the administration of construction sites, so products and services in the supply of food, consultancy, working tools supply, maintenance services and equipments, security services, information technology, and labour are included.

Related to construction are other great opportunities such as equipments supply; construction, maintenance and improvement of roads, airports, railways, stadiums, and buildings; law specialists for property expropriation just to cite few.

In the information technology sector communication services and projects are also included. Probably the major investments will be in the communications projects and implementation areas once the country must be ready to receive and accommodate several media experts and broadcasting equipments. Due to this necessity, those working with consultancy projects; IT maintenance and implementation;

television broadcasting services; technical support; software developments; data communication etc are some who can take advantage of the investments in this sector.

Tourism may be the sector that will take the most of the investments being made once Brazil will be shown to millions, probably billions of people around the world. This will likely increase the interest travellers will have in the country during and after the events. Major investments in hotel rooms' construction and improvements must be made, especially in certain host cities that still lack rooms to receive fans and travellers, and surrounding hosting touristic cities. Restaurants and entertainment places, products and services are also in need and may be of great opportunity.

Other areas and activities related to tourism include travel agencies and transportation services; entertainment events organization services; labour specialization and training services; food and beverage supply; wellness services; security services etc.

Agribusiness in Brazil is a very competitive, efficient, and modern sector in terms of the international market. There are still many opportunities available prior to the 2014 World Cup and 2016 Olympics and following these major sporting events. Of the investments related to the 2014 World Cup and 2016 Olympics, food production is still the most appealing opportunity and with it comes other types of investments that can be worth a look. The investment in machinery and technology is still advancing in

Brazil which brings opportunities for firms and companies to establish themselves in this sector, or in the international trade of machinery for both selling and renting. As the demand for machinery increases, the need for specialized technical knowledge about mechanics and operations will also go up. Veterinary services are also required.

Technical knowledge and expertise in cultivation techniques are also required, bringing with it financial, negotiation, and international trade consultancy services. The opportunity with agribusiness in Brazil may be more appealing also for the long term. As an example, according to the Brazilian Agricultural Ministry, by 2030 Brazil is expected to provide one in every three agribusiness products produced in the world.

When it comes to sports and entertainment, Brazil is also another good place to be. Not only because of the coming events, but also because the country still lacks specialized businesses and companies in this industry. It seems the world of entertainment is opening to Brazil, and Brazil is opening to the entertainment industry. Until now, the biggest sporting events Brazil hosted were the 1950 World Cup, annual Formula 1 races in Rio de Janeiro and Sao Paulo, and the 2007 Pan-American Games in Rio de Janeiro. After Brazil and Rio de Janeiro were selected for the 2014 World Cup and 2016 Olympic Games respectively, a series of other major sporting events were selected to go to the country. Just to give some examples, in 2013, Brazil will host the Confederations Cup and an edition of the X-Games.

From 2014 on, the country will also have an ATP 500 (tennis) tournament, and in 2019 is time for soccer again with the Copa America. For this reason, consultancy in sports business and marketing, sporting events, and arenas and clubs administration will be even more in demand. The same happens to the entertainment industry. Sports medicine is another area which will offer great investment opportunities.

Finally, sustainability is also offering great business opportunities in Brazil. With the huge activity in the construction industry, these opportunities can be even greater. Consultancy in sustainable projects which may help improve the usage of solar energy, rain water re-usage, and many others is being required to support the construction companies that offer this type of products and services. With this type of opportunity comes the demand for specific knowledge and services to support and contribute to the construction sector. Another major area that can also increase in Brazil in the next years is in recycling centres and programs.

As a developing country Brazil also offers a really big number of opportunities in many other industries such as oil and energy. With all the changes being made, Brazil is expected to offer a much better infrastructure for companies and investors interested in the country which may lead to an array of post event opportunities. Of course everybody involved in the business world is aware of what the opportunities may be, and the intent of this book is to bring some other areas that may not be as clear as others.

Chapter 15: Environmental Industries Sector in Brazil

There is US$10 billion of investment into new solid waste infrastructure, driven by increased tonnage of waste and Brazil's 2010 National Policy on Solid Waste.

Market overview

Brazil is the 5th largest country in world by total area and population, the most industrialised nation in Latin America and the 6th largest world economy. With a GDP of US$2.5 trillion in 2011. As a high-growth market there is huge potential across many sectors for foreign businesses.

Brazil has the world's largest reserves of tropical forest, biodiversity and flows of fresh water (25%). Brazil also has the largest underground reservoir (Guarani Aquifer). In addition, Brazil has a strong science base, is a keen promoter of technology transfer, and is a world leader in bio-fuel technologies.

Brazil's National Growth Acceleration Programme ("PAC Plan"), launched in 2007, has driven investments in the areas of energy, transport, housing and sanitation. As part of the plan's second phase, the Brazilian government estimates that roughly US$13.4 billion (R$25.2 billion) will be spent on sanitation between 2011 and 2014.

In addition, the construction programmes for the development of the sports events 2014 FIFA World Cup and 2016 Olympic Games will drive sustainable management plan frameworks.

Brazil offers exciting business opportunities for those looking to expand into its dynamic marketplace, particularly in the environment and water sector.

Key opportunities

There is a wide-range of factors driving investment in Environmental Goods & Services (EG&S):

- An increasing number of companies with environmental management systems.
- Adoption of international standards of environmental performance by exporters and multinational companies.
- New legislation framework such as the National Policy on Solid Waste.

Brazilian businesses are fully aware that their competitiveness is tied to improving management of their social and environmental impacts. In that sense, private companies are actively looking for low carbon solutions.

Solid Waste

US$10 billion of investment into new solid waste infrastructure, driven by increased tonnage of waste and Brazil's 2010 National Policy on Solid Waste:

- Recycling and treatment facilities which involves the collection, sorting, reprocessing and reintegration of materials.
- Reduction, which includes process innovations, sustainable designs, and lightweight, low-material packaging.
- Intelligent re-use and sorting techniques (such as industrial symbiosis).
- Technologies that improve the thermal content of waste.
- Finding opportunities for AD (for instance, sewage sludge and farm slurry).

Air Pollution Control

- Advanced stack emission control.
- Stack monitoring and testing equipment (particularly continuous emission monitoring).
- Atmospheric monitoring and testing equipment.
- Flammable gas-detection equipment.

Soil Remediation and Groundwater Treatment Control

- On-site investigation, sampling and analysis.
- Latest soil washing technologies.
- Enhancing in-country technology with incremental improvements.

Brazil's environment and water sector presents vast opportunities to foreign companies. It is fundamental to understand the market before positioning products and services for market entry. Opportunities are likely to outweigh risks, particularly as business contracts in Brazil are often based on trust and acceptability, thus negating the need for companies to revert to legal instruments to resolve cases of dissent or disagreement.

Chapter 16: Creative Industries Sector in Brazil

Boosting the Creative Industries sector is one of the main goals of the Brazilian Ministry for Culture. Britain's tradition of innovation and global cultural connections are highly regarded in Brazil. A Creative Industries Secretariat was created in January 2011 by President Dilma Roussef to increase the participation of this sector in the Brazilian economy.

Market overview

Recent studies showed that Creative Industries account for 2.5% of Brazil's GDP. Some states, such as Sao Paulo and Rio de Janeiro, have already achieved shares above the country's average in this sector. The estimated turnover of the sector for 2010 was of US$240 billion. Between 2002 and 2008, the Brazilian exports of goods and services in this segment went from US$ 2.4 billion to US$ 7.5 billion.

Creative Industries are growing at a faster rate than the world economy in general, representing seven percent of global GDP, equivalent to US$1.3 billion dollars. (Source: UNCTAD). In Brazil, the segment grew 500% over a period of 10 years, generating around 1.8 million new jobs. Until 2010, the core of the Creative Industries sector employed 771,000 workers. However, the entire Creative Industries chain which comprises industry, services and trade accounted for 11.8 million jobs, most of them concentrated on fashion and design. In Brazil, the number of companies in this segment exceeds 320,000. 99.87% of them are small and medium companies.

Key opportunities

Brazil is the world's 12th music market. Between 2010 and 2011, the recording industry grew 8.47%, achieving a turnover of 129.5 million GBP. Opportunities for electronic, British and American pop music can be found throughout the country.

Between 2008 and 2010, the book publishing industry in Brazil went through a fast growth, going from approximately 340.000 books published to around 492.000. Their earnings in 2010 were around 1.56 billion GBP. Also, the last edition of Book Bienal reached an audience of 670,000 people.

Design and fashion design are others sub-sectors of Creative Industries that offer major commercial opportunities for UK companies. Brazilian companies are fully aware of the necessity to invest in design in order to compete overseas and Brazil wants to increase its exports of sophisticated products. Also, the country's luxury market, where UK fashion designers fit, is the largest in Latin America, accounting for 70% of the segment.

Opportunities in this field are distributed along seven promising cities in addition to Sao Paulo and Rio de Janeiro. In 2012, another luxury landmark will be inaugurated in Sao Paulo; JK Mall. This shopping centre will be home to the first Topshop store in Brazil.

The major sports events that Brazil will host in the next years (2014 World Cup and 2016 Olympics in Rio) will propel the role of art, culture and Creative Industries in general. New ideas, especially in services, design, branding and marketing, will certainly be explored.

The creative industries sector in Brazil has no specific key method for doing business. The best way to approach the market is to be introduced to it in all of Brazil from the North to the South, paying special attention to the Southern region, where the cities of Sao Paulo and Rio de Janeiro are located. Salvador and Curitiba also present good opportunities.

UK products are considered to be of high quality but also high price. In most cases, the decisive issue still is the price. Under Brazilian's law, it is mandatory to have marketing literature in Portuguese. Brazilians are well-versed in international trading practices and trends.

Because of the dynamics of the Brazilian market, the businessmen are quick decision-makers, extremely flexible and fast to detect commercial opportunities. The initial approach when doing business is extremely important.

Brazilians expect face-to-face contact with their suppliers and look for commitment to their market. Clear catalogue prices in US dollars FOB or preferably landed at a Brazilian port. When visiting Brazil, despite the tropical climate in much of the country, it is customary to wear a suit and tie.

Chapter 17: Life Sciences Sector in Brazil

Brazil has the largest healthcare and medical devices market in Latin America. Healthcare is mainly provided by the state, but private partners in this sector have quickly increased their investments over the last eight years.

Market overview

With an annual healthcare expenditure expected to be of USD 305 million by 2015, and 6,801 hospitals and 371,000 medical doctors, representing 4.05% of the world's total Brazil is simply a market too big to ignore.

Brazil is growing rapidly and is expected to become the world's 5th largest economy by 2030. In line with this growth, the healthcare market in the country is expected to grow at a compound annual growth rate of 35% for the next ten years (compared to the global average rate of 4.1%), driven by increasing opportunities in the sector. By 2015 the value of the market is estimated to be approximately £85 billion.

The key drivers for this growth forecast are the higher purchasing power of the low and middle classes, the higher life expectancy of the general population, the higher population, and the growth in the home care market. FIFA 2014 World Cup and the Olympic

Games in 2016 will also drive government investments to the healthcare sector, starting in 2012.

The pharmaceutical industry corresponds to 2% of the global sales market and is the 10th amongst world leaders in the sector. The Brazilian pharmaceutical industry is comprised of 553 companies, more than 50,000 pharmacies and more than 500 distributors of pharmaceutical products; the largest market in LA in 2008 with £7Bi sales (39.6% share of the Latin American market).

Key opportunities

- High end medical devices: mostly all of the low-tech medical technology is produced domestically, but for high-end and novel technologies the consumer market has to look overseas.

- E-health and remote diagnostics: The Brazilian public health system, along with the private sector, is investing in remote access for a large share of the population through e-health technology, which will expand the universal coverage to more people.

- Medical education and training: The economic growth the country expects will have an impact on its education sector. Many Brazilian institutions such as universities and others are keen to sign deals with foreign universities and the market is huge for the various prestigious UK degrees, especially for the

MDN education where partnerships were not yet made.

The Brazilian government establishes specific regulations for the registration, licensing and/or exemption of Life Sciences products. The National Health Surveillance Agency – ANVISA was established in 1999 to improve the health protection of the population by exercising sanitary control over the production and commercialisation of products and services subject to sanitary surveillance. The role of ANVISA is equivalent to the role of the MHRA in the UK. In order to export and distribute products in Brazil, foreign companies must either establish a local manufacturing unit, a local office or appoint a Brazilian partner to hold the registration with ANVISA.

The selection of the right partner is essential for the success of your company in Brazil. A Brazilian person or company must have a Company Working Allowance certificate, issued by ANVISA, to become your Brazilian Registration Holder (BRH). It is common for distributors to be the BRH, but there are also registration holding companies and consultants specialised in holding ANVISA licences. This permit allows your local partner to import, distribute, store and sell the product in Brazil. This point of contact in Brazil will be considered as the legal representative of the exporting company in the country.

Chapter 18: Mass Transport Sector in Brazil

Brazil will receive a total of BRL 443 billion in investments for port, road, rail, urban mobility and airport projects until 2016.

Market overview

Brazil is one of the world's fastest-growing economies. In order to cope with its new scenario, which demands investments in logistics, urban mobility and improvements on airports, the country is investing BRL 443 billion until 2016 to improve its transport system, mainly envisaging the deadline of hosting the 2014 World Cup and the 2016 Olympic Games.

After a long time focusing investments in the road sector, neglecting other modal systems such as ports, airports and railways, the Brazilian government is now giving priority to implementing and upgrading mass transport projects as well as extending private participation through concession in infrastructure operations and investments.

Key opportunities

Railways

Cargo and passenger railway transport in Brazil is facing a new cycle of investments, which could comprise more than BRL 110 billion coming from both the public and private sectors. The richest Brazilian state alone, São Paulo, is investing BRL 30 billion until 2015 for the expansion of its passenger railway systems. Currently, there are 4 expansion projects under construction.

Rio de Janeiro city is also building two new metro lines and improving the commuter railway system. Cities such as Belo Horizonte and Salvador will expand their existing metro networks, while Curitiba and Porto Alegre in the south of Brazil are set to build entirely new ones.

The Federal government is discussing the possibility to build the first high speed train in Brazil. The project is designed to connect the two largest Brazilian cities, São Paulo and Rio de Janeiro. After two redesigns, the tender for this project is expected to be issued be end of 2012.

Airports

Brazil has experienced an increase of 153% in passenger air traffic between 2003 and 2011, from 71.2 million/year in 2003 to 180 million/year in 2011. The Brazilian government had to seek new financing sources for the airport sector, opening the market for private operators.

The first privatisation round involved three airports being Guarulhos (São Paulo), Viracopos (São Paulo) and Brasília (capital of Brazil) where the Federal government (Infraero) has kept 49% stake. The new owners must invest BRL 16.2 billion to improve the operations and facilities. On the other hand the Federal government will invest more than BRL 3.5 billion in the airports remaining under its full control and that are located in the 2014 World Cup host cities.

Ports

The port sector in Brazil will receive more than BRL 30 billion in investments, of which BRL 9.5 billion are set to come from the Federal government and BRL 21 billion from the private sector. These investments will be allocated to building new ports and also to extend and improve existing ones.

At the ports of Itaguaí (Rio de Janeiro state) and Vila do Conde (Pará state); investments will reach BRL 1.5 billion and BRL 1.3 billion respectively to build new terminals.

About 77 ports will have their concession contracts revised as they are about to finish next year and, if appropriate, they might become available for bidding processes to new interested concessionaires.

Chapter 19: Fire and Security Sector in Brazil

The Brazilian fire and security market had a turnover of R$1.2bn (at FOB values) in 2011 according to the SIA (Security Industry of America) annual survey. The market is expected to grow at the rate of 20.6% per year, reaching R$3.7bn by 2017, driven by investments in infrastructure, oil and gas, public security and sports installations. (£ = R$3.06 May 2012).

Market overview

There is an estimated 10,000 EPS (electronic physical security) companies in Brazil. 39.6% of the market is for TV/video surveillance, 20.8% access control systems, 19.2% intruder control, 10.4% fire detection and 10% electronic article surveillance. 55.6% of products are imported and 44.4% made locally. The residential sector makes up 9.1% of the total market and generates demand mostly for intrusion alarm systems as well as access control systems and, in some cases, video systems. The products used in this segment generally are in the low-cost category. The principal factor in the recent rapid market growth has been the increase in property crime, which has generated a general feeling of insecurity in the population.

The non-residential segment, 90.9% of the market, includes the public sector (government and institutions) and the private sector (industries such as retail, tourism, financial services and others). The main product opportunities for UK suppliers are in technologically advanced niche products, such as those with the latest digital technology, wireless and biometrics systems.

The 2014 World Cup and the 2016 Olympics will be held in Brazil and this will increase demand for security products in related sectors, such as construction, housing, hotels and tourism. In the public sector the federal government has predicted an extra budget in 2012 of R$717m for investment in the security sector. The main goal is the strengthening of the public security forces, civil defence and the fire brigade in the light of the major sporting events.

Key opportunities

World Cup 2014: 12 cities and venues during the competition. Security products and technologies will be required for venues, airports, and other transport infrastructure.

Olympics 2016: Security products and technologies will be required for venues, airports, and other transport infrastructure, mainly for Rio de Janeiro but also for Sao Paulo and other Olympic locations.

The exploration of pre-salt oil fields will also be a significant factor for growth, following the major oil finds off the coast of Rio de Janeiro and Sao Paulo.

The other main sectors of opportunity are in the industrial sector; oil production, refining (15 refineries) and distribution; energy installations; banking (17,000 agencies); hotels; the public sector (65 airports, prisons, trains and underground); ports; shopping centres and other commerce; residential condominiums; communications (mobile and corporate services infrastructure); and hospitals.

Relatively low penetration of security equipment in comparison with US and European markets means that there is scope for growth in the supply of security equipment to businesses of all kinds. Many local suppliers are turning to China and the Far East to replace their own production. However, there is still potential for the expansion of the local manufacturing base with tax incentives to electronics companies. Currently, there are few manufacturers of electronic security equipment although software is developed locally. Brazil manufactures sensors, alarm centres, monitoring and access systems and non-electronic products such as automatic doors and gates, safes, locks and casings.

Brazil is heavily dependent on electronics imports and the revaluation of the Brazilian currency in recent years has encouraged imports. A large proportion of products from Europe are supplied via the USA, where the large volumes permit good discounts. US manufacturers have a presence in Brazil through distributors, agents or manufacturing. Israel, Japan, Canada, Germany, UK and Italy are also important suppliers but Taiwan, Korea and especially China have increased their share considerably in recent years with relatively cheap products.

Chapter 20: Education Sector in Brazil

Improving the education in Brazil is one of the objectives of the Brazilian Government, with national programmes that adapt new techniques to the classroom. The private sector is also booming with new investments.

Market overview

The Brazilian educational system is predominately public. Public schools and Universities are entirely free. In the last ten years the percentage of school-age children enrolled in public schools has steadily increased and the private sector's share has declined sharply, with the exception of higher education.

Brazil has the highest return on education among the 17 Latin American countries. Also, the return on higher education in Brazil is higher than that in countries such as Argentina and Taiwan.

Young Brazilians are better educated, more familiar with English language and very keen to invest in the education and training sector.

Middle class Brazilians are increasing their expenses with education, going from 8% - 10% to 15% - 17% of their total income between 2010 and 2011.

In the past years there has been an increase of workers with higher education and post graduation courses. There has also been a major change in the corporate culture in Brazil. Companies fully accept that staff needs enhanced skills, including English.

Brazil recognises the need to upgrade and modernise its system of vocational education. Recent studies show that the country lacks qualified workers in many sectors, such as industry, in which 69% of the companies are affected by that. Some sectors, such as construction, consider the lack of qualified workers as their main challenge to expand.

The British NVQ and SVQ systems are becoming better known and respected in the Ministry of Education.

Brazilian educational institutions are generally open to the idea of international partnerships, which are seen as providing business benefits and added status to the internal market.

Key opportunities

Massive training and re-training in several sectors of the Brazilian economy namely in the telecom, healthcare, oil and gas, construction, retail and financial sectors.

Technological equipment is in demand. Brazil is anxious to purchase software and other associated equipment (ICT for education)

Distance learning: because of the vast geography of the country (8.5 million sq km), distance education has the potential to reach those areas outside the main urban centres where education provision is weakest. **MBAs:** especially in management training and business administration.

In Sao Paulo alone there are 10,000 companies and organisations that run in-house and out-of-house training programmes. There are opportunities for foreign companies offering training assistance.

Special educational needs: where the Brazilian government should invest in the next few years. A special need is an area that is growing quite fast.

The route to the market will depend on the kind of product and service to be offered. As Brazil is a large and diverse country, the most common is to work with a business partner with strong commercial links in different Brazilian regions.

In terms of cultural standards Brazilians are well informed business people and brand orientated. Personal relationship is fundamental to find success in Brazil and in most cases is recommended that the company sends a representative to have face to face meetings when approaching the market.

Chapter 21: Consumer Goods Sector in Brazil

The Brazilian Consumer Goods sector is one of the biggest in Latin America with a stable economy that grew 2.7% in 2011 becoming the 6th largest economy in the world.

Market overview

The strong domestic demand continues to drive the performance of the consumer goods sector.

The rise of the middle class, which doubled in the last 10 years, and the increasing in the purchase power has boosted the Brazilian Retail Trade Volume Index.

This created opportunities for UK companies working in the consumer goods sector that have the products, which this large and highly urban population of 200 million is keen to buy.

Key opportunities

Despite the world crisis, Brazilian GDP had an average growth rate of 4.5% from 2006 to 2010, compared to 2.7% in the previous five years.

Consumers and businesses have developed higher standards both for quality and value for money and Brazil has the largest middle class in Latin America with an appetite for quality goods and services every bit as demanding as the consumers in London, Paris or New York.

Respecting this consumption scenario, there are opportunities for European and US companies in the following areas:

Food and Drink: Brazilian Food and Drink Sector is one of the most competitive in Latin America and is has emerged as one of the leading suppliers in the global food industry.

Cosmetic: Brazil is the world's third largest beauty market just after Japan and USA. Brazilian women are 100% beauty conscious and spent US$ 3.7 billion on beauty products in 2011.

Luxury goods: Brazilian luxury market had a turnover of US$ 10 billion in 2011, which represented an increase of 11.5% compared to 2010. Brazilians usually spend 1,215 (GBP) every time they go shopping. A new Shopping Centre named JK is opened in Sao Paulo with the following luxury brands: Prada, Gucci, Carolina Herrera, Lanvin and Chanel. Burberry, Aston Martin, and Bentley to name a few are already extremely successful in Brazil.

Fashion, Clothing and Accessories, according to ABIT(Brazilin Textile and Apparel Association) the textile, fashion and clothing sector's turnover of 2011 was of US$ 51 billion. Zara, C&A and UK fashion designers such as Issa, Stella McCartney are presented in Brazil. TopShop is opening at JK Shopping Centre and H&M is researching the market.

On the Consumer Goods sector there is not a specific model or best route to be followed.

The best way into the Brazilian market will really depend on the mix of products or services to be exported.

Most UK companies work through distributors, importers and local representatives.

Depending on the product or service offered it can be either through a national or local distribution contract. The majority of Brazilian importers ask for exclusivity when it comes to luxury goods for instance.

Franchise is another route to the Brazilian market so as the partnerships with experienced local players.

To establish an operation or sell into a multi-brand store in a local shopping centre is also perceived as a successful way to enter Brazil. On line shopping is also growing fast in Brazil.

Trade barrier: The strongest barriers for the consumer goods sector in general are taxes, customs bureaucracy and complex labour laws. Taxes applied on imports can raise a product's cost up to 108%.

Regulatory standards: on the food and drink and cosmetics sectors, foreign companies should be made aware that they need prior approval from ANVISA, which is the Brazilian Regulatory Agency created in 1999 to protect Brazilian population.

The Brazilian government establishes specific regulations and licensing for food, drink and cosmetics products.

In terms of cultural standards Brazilians are well informed business people and brand orientated. Brazilians are very sophisticated consumers, well travelled and fully aware of what the world can offer.

Chapter 22: Leisure and Tourism Sector in Brazil

Brazil is the 7th destination in the world in number of international events, and was chosen to host the 2014 World Cup and the Olympic Games in 2016.

Market overview

With the end of 2010, the domestic tourism industry began to indicate a time of great expectation of future earnings. With the favourable economic climate in recent years, which combined GDP growth, increased foreign direct investment in the country, higher inflation control, greater availability of credit and gradual fall in interest rates, a favourable scenario was established for the development of national tourism.

In addition, the tourist sector in Brazil is "piggybacking" on the current growth of the middle class and in the major events that will take place in the coming years as the FIFA World Cup 2014 and the Olympic Games Rio 2016.

Latest data shows that in 2011 Brazil received 4 million tourists, whom spent US$ 6,775 billion.

In 2010 the 80 biggest Brazilian tourism companies had a turnover of R$ 42.8 billion (£16.17 billion) and employed around 96,000 people.

Tourism accounts for 3% of Brazil's GDP and forecasts are that by 2020 will be responsible for 8%. (Source: Ministry of Tourism).

Currently, the sector employs 7.2 million. For the World Cup in 2014 there will be around 870,000 professionals dealing directly with the public and visitors in general. The Ministry of Tourism predicts that the sector's turnover will increase by 16.5% in 2014.

Key opportunities

Since Brazil was chosen to host the 2014 World Cup and Olympic Games in 2016, the Ministry of Tourism started a Project to develop 65 destinations and turn them into a model of high tourism quality before 2014.

Such initiatives refer to vocational courses to World Cup staff, in areas such as tourism, languages, lodging, security, health and IT. This aims to provide qualified workers of top destinations during the World Cup.

Forecasts are that Brazil will receive 8 million visitors in 2014, 600 thousand of which should arrive during the World Cup month.

In the infrastructure sector, the Brazilian government approved so far projects that together will cost U$1.48 billion.

As regards to leisure, until 2010 live events were focused only on classes A and B. Average ticket price goes from U$138 – 300. For these events to survive in Brazil, the sector will have to offer new options to its public, such as strongly invest in class C. Average ticket should cost U$12 to attract this ascending class.

Investment in music in Brazil is growing quite fast and this represents opportunities for foreign Company in the leisure sector.

Museums and Attractions are other important areas that foreign companies should exploit; from security to content. A new museum named "Museu da Pessoa" will be built in Sao Paulo especially for the World Cup in 2014. This is an initiative from Jaime Lerner, architect from Curitiba.

There is not a specific way to enter the Brazilian market in the tourism and leisure sectors. This will really depend on the kind of product and service to be offered. The recommendation is for foreign companies to partner with well established local players.

Chapter 23: Financial and Legal Services in Brazil

This country that most of us probably only know for their national soccer team and beautiful beaches is definitely also worth to look at from an economic point of view. The country is currently the world's 6th largest economy and the largest economy of South America. It already has well-developed agriculture, manufacturing, mining and service sectors. Brazil's industry is very diverse, ranging from manufacturers of aircrafts to petrochemicals. Furthermore, it is one of the few countries in the world that are energy self-sufficient. This country is also part of the so-called BRIC countries, an acronym for the countries (Brazil, Russia, India and China) that according to many experts will overtake the G7 economies by 2027.

Brazil has vast natural resources, a rising middle class, an increasing consumption pattern backed by Governmental policies and a developed industrial base. Further to that, Brazil is a stable democracy with a booming economy.

Market overview

As the largest single economy in the region, the state of the Brazilian economy and the value of its currency have great influence on other economies in the region. The Stock Exchange in São Paulo (Bovespa) is by far and away the most important in Latin America. If s foreign financial services companies can succeed in Brazil, it will have far reaching consequences for their success in the rest of the region.

Brazil is currently a relatively open market for financial services, with still a few exception areas such as legal services. As an emerging market, fluctuations in the fortunes of the economy frequently occur. The principal factor affecting conditions in the near future are the challenges to continue to promote sustainable growth in a period of continued global economic slowdown and unstable market conditions.

Insurance and Reinsurance

The steady rise of the middle class along with increased incomes levels has led to more demand for different lines of insurance products including home, automotive, life and causality. Places formerly seen as marginalised, like the outskirts in Rio and/or the poor communities in Sao Paulo, are now being regarded as a very fertile ground for business. Also the opening of the reinsurance market and gradual dissolution of the state monopoly has created a space for experienced multinational companies to fill the current void.

Public Private Partnerships (PPP)

In Latin America alone, it is estimated that in the next 5 years US$70 billion will be needed in infrastructure development. More than two thirds is expected to be channelled to Brazilian backed regional projects like the Transoceanic Road linking Brazil and Peru. The role of PPPs in Brazil has greatly increased in importance given the need to detach financial mechanisms from the development bank BNDES as a means not to impact the country's fiscal sustainability. The upcoming 2014 World Cup and 2016 Olympic Games will present PPP business opportunities.

Carbon Market

The developing carbon market in Brazil is providing opportunities for British expertise to cash in on the growing demand, as joint-ventures, and consulting partnerships can be of mutual benefit to both parties. The newly established (December 2011) BVRio has been created to enable trading of environmental commodities through an exchange.

Venture Capital/Private Equity

Venture capital/private equity has shown tremendous opportunity for direct investment from abroad. As the number of business opportunities arises in Brazil, so has the need for funding. As a fundamental instrument in the development of emerging markets, PE/VC has been of huge importance to the Brazilian economy.

There are three reasons to invest in Brazil now:

1. The middle class of Brazil's population is growing at a rapid rate accompanied by a growth in disposable income, which will lead to more domestic demand.

2. Rising price of commodities, a profitable situation for countries like Brazil that have huge both precious and industrial metals.

3. The Brazilian government encourages Real Estate and Foreign Investment. Foreign property investment has only very few restrictions and therefore is developing at an incredible pace knowing that there is a high demand for housing in Brazil.

For those of you who want to invest in Brazil there are multiple options. An easy way to invest is by participating in one of the many mutual funds focused on the Brazilian economy. Another way to invest is to buy so-called trackers of the main Brazilian index, the Bovespa. There is a great chance that both investment options will focus mostly on Brazilian companies, like Vale or Petrobas. Although these companies might be very profitable on the short-term I don't think they are interesting for investors with a longer investment horizon. When you want to invest by buying individual shares I recommend that you buy the ones of domestically oriented companies. Here are my top 3:

1. Brasil Foods [BRSF] is Brazil's leading provider of processed, brand name foods and meatpacker. The company is also a major exporter of meat to Asia, Russia and the Middle East.

2. Gafisa [GFA] builds houses for a wide target group, from middle class apartments to expensive villas. Besides the core business they also offer mortgages. An annual growth rate of 60% over the

last 5 years and more cash than outstanding debt are two interesting factors to consider.

3. Companhia Brasileira de Distribucao [CBD] owns the leading national supermarket chain and different electronics and appliances retailers.

Legal Service Sector

The legal services sector in Brazil is considerably more protectionist when compared to the UK's. The Federal Bar Association in Brazil (OAB Federal) enacted a Resolution in 2000 which restricts the entrance and operations of foreign law firms (British included). However, there are still some profitable opportunities for British business in the Brazilian legal services sector. English law is still reasonably used in Brazil, particularly in relation to international trade and insurance/reinsurance contracts.

It is important to take a medium to long term view, as success in Brazil requires commitment and patience. Many global players are present in the country and some sort of local presence is preferred. Even so there are niche areas of expertise where there is significant scope for operating remotely from the UK, requiring only periodical visits to the market.

The market is moderately liberal and there are opportunities for investment by commercial banks through purchase/joint-venture with existing Brazilian banks. Other service providers may find that local association or partnership, where permitted, is the best way to approach the market, particularly to benefit from the market knowledge and network already established. Some form of local presence is vital to doing business in Brazil, and strongly recommended.

Chapter 24: Food and Drink Opportunities in Brazil

Brazil is one of the world's leading producers of agricultural products and foodstuffs. In the last years, Brazil has become the world's largest exporter of beef, soybeans, coffee, orange juice, sugar and chicken. Brazil Food and Drink sector is one of the most competitive in the region and has emerged as one of the leading suppliers in the global food industry. According to data supplied by MAPA, the Brazilian Ministry of Agriculture, in 2010 agribusiness exports went up to US$76,441 billion.

Functional food

Currently Brazil is among the largest consumers of nutritional food and vitamins, with a total year amount of US$18billion. This is due not only to the level of maturity and information of the Brazilian average consumer, but also a reflection of the income growth.

Some of the major players in this segment in Brazil are Danone (Activia), Nestlé (Sollys) and local brands Seven Boys, Bimbo and Nutrella (breads).

Food Service

In the last decade food service presented a growth of 219%, due to the greater participation of women in the work place, new consumption habits and the growth of economy. It is heading towards accounting for approximately 50% of the Brazilian food industry. The major players in this segment are Sadia and Perdigão.

Organics

In Latin America, Brazil and Argentina produce the majority of organic products.

In 1999, the estimated consumption in Brazil was of US$150million. Production of organic products shows a yearly growth rate between 30% and 50%. In 2004 there were approximately 14,000 organic manufacturers.

In 2010 72 companies that are members of Organics Brasil totalled US$108.2million in exports, representing a growth of 130% compared to 2009.

For the Olympic Games in Brazil in 2014 the plans are that only organic food will be served. Soon Brazil will be among the world's top prodcuers of organic food.

Supermarket Retail

The top three supermarket chain in Brazil, Pão de Açúcar, Carrefour and Wal-Mart respectively, are responsible for 50% of all food products sold in Brazil. Some of them even provide the seeds to be planted.

Drinks

Likewise, in the drinks sector, consumption has grown proportionally as spending power increases. Also, the sector is sensitive to seasonal changes. When it comes to drinks sector in Brazil, the hotter the weather, the better. The major competitor for beers is Ambev and for soft drinks is Coca-Cola.

Niche areas for imported food and drink are premium branded products, speciality food and drink products, food ingredients, and diet and light range of products.

Chapter 25: Construction Opportunities in Brazil

Brazil is the largest country in South America, both in geographical and commercial terms. As a high-growth market there is huge potential across many sectors.

The construction sector accounts for approximately 13% of Brazil's GDP and grew approximately 11.6% in 2010, compared to the 7.5% growth of the country's GDP. The building materials sector alone grew over 12% in 2010. Such impressive growth rates show that the Brazilian construction sector is facing its best performance ever.

The Accelerated Growth Programme (known as "PAC Plan") launched in 2007 has driven investments in the areas of energy, transport, housing and sanitation. In addition, the construction programmes for the development of the 2014 FIFA World Cup and 2016 Olympic Games are seen as the main driver for opening up a wide range of opportunities for foreign companies in the areas of construction services and goods.

There are several large architectural, construction and engineering companies in Brazil which offer internationally recognised competitiveness but there is potential for foreign companies to partner with Brazilian firms in specific projects in the areas below:

According to official statistics, Brazil has a housing deficit of around 5.8 million family homes. It will be necessary for the country to build 23.5 million homes until 2022. In March 2009, President Lula announced the long-awaited ambitious housing package to spend £27 billion per year until 2014 to support a large federal housing programme called "Minha Casa, Minha Vida". This package includes a number of positive measures mostly addressed to the low-income segment.

The real estate market in Brazil remained stable during the global credit crisis of 2009, and is now projected to expand further due to investments and the rising income of the Brazilian middle class. Since 2004 developers, banks and consumers have been investing in Brazil's major cities and on the beaches along the country's North-eastern, South-eastern and Southern coasts in holiday homes, luxury apartments, resorts, shopping malls, commercial building and residential complexes. Investments in the sector in 2009 reached £58 billion and grew further in 2010 reaching £70 billion according to studies launched by the construction trade association and a private research institute. In São Paulo, there was an average valorisation of 175% regarding new buildings between 2000 and 2010.

The luxury market in Brazil, (those families with income over £8,500/month), accounts for only 0.27% of the population, however it is a market which spends over £770 million pounds per year on property. This market is concentrated in Sao Paulo and Rio de Janeiro, for both commercial and private buildings. A recent study showed that Rio de Janeiro, São Paulo, Brasília and Salvador are listed among the 10 most expensive squared metres in the country. According to a recent international study, São Paulo city is the 5th biggest market for high class corporate buildings in the world.

The shopping centre industry is also an important segment that should be closely watched due to rapid growth. According to the Brazilian Shopping Centre Industry (Abrasce) the market accounts for 18.3% of Brazilian retail and 2% of the country's GDP. The industry ended 2010 with a total revenue of approximately £33 billion and an 11% growth rate over 2010.

There are currently around 408 malls in the country, with an early year prediction of 24 new malls to be constructed in 2011.

In Brazil, the tourism sector as a whole accounts for roughly 6% of the country's GDP, registering an average annual growth rate of 10% in the past few years and the hotel industry remains attractive. Out of the total investment in this sector, 50% originates in the country itself, and 50% come from abroad.

Hotel groups from Portugal, Spain and France have increased their investments, and other major international hotel chains are expected to invest in the country. The Northeast seems to be the main destination for investments; the Ministry of Tourism predicts the private sector will invest approximately £3.5 billion until 2019 in the region. Despite the

Brazilian market looking at huge investments in the northeast region, companies will also keep investing in Rio de Janeiro, Sao Paulo, Belo Horizonte and other host cities of the FIFA World Cup 2014. The Brazilian Development Bank, BNDES, alongside the Ministry of Tourism have developed a credit line for the tourism sector of over £380 million, specifically designated to construction, enhancement and to encourage entrepreneurship.

Rio de Janiero's world famous football stadium Maracana, which used to hold just under 200,000 standing spectators, when it was first built for the 1950 World Cup, is in the process of being re-built to house 85,000 seated spectators and fulfil all FIFA's security specifications .

It is scheduled to be ready in 2013 well in time for the World Cup final in July 13th 2014 but there is a report out that the stadium has suffered an explosion with one worker reported dead and other workers striking complaining about working conditions.

Maracana is one of twelve stadiums being upgraded or built from scratch around Brazil in readiness for the World Cup – Manaus, Fortaleza, Natal, Recife, Salvador, Cuiaba, Brasilia, Belo Horizonte, Porto Alegre, Rio de Janeiro, Sao Paulo, Curitiba and a total of approximately £660 million has been put aside for the repair, upgrading and construction of the stadiums of which three are privately owned.

Certainly there are huge opportunities for foreign companies to be part of the huge World Cup and

Olympics in 2016 but it will be part of the lower supply chain for the massive infrastructure upgrading which needs to take place. The window of opportunity is amazingly beginning to close as so many companies from around the world are already moving in on Brazil as they scent profits now and in the future.

Corporate Buildings Under Construction (Top 5 cities worldwide) m²(million) Dec (2009) Moscow 3.91 Guangzhou 3.12 Dubai 2.16 Shanghai 2.13 São Paulo 1.44.

Chapter 26:
Telecommunications
Opportunities in Brazil

The telecommunications sector is expected to grow strongly in 2011, driven by strong sales of smart phones and investments in infrastructure in the sector.

The main issues in the telecommunications market in 2011 following the market consolidation in 2009-2010 are services convergence; take-up of smart-phones and 3G expansion; number portability; IPTV; Digital TV; Wimax; broadband expansion and government promotion of broadband access for all; regulation for MVNO services.

There were 205m mobile lines in March 2011, up from 191.5m in September 2010, making Brazil the fifth largest market in the world.

Opportunities

Market consolidation has left 4 major telecommunications groups:

Mobile operator Vivo has been taken over completely by Telefonica after the acquisition of the 50% share owned by Portugal Telecom.

Telefonica is also the leading fixed operator and owns TVA, the leading Pay-TV provider, as well as Speedy (internet and broadband).

Portugal Telecom has bought into Oi/Brasil Telecom, the Brazilian group in which the Brazilian government is a major shareholder. Oi was the first consolidated and converged services provider.

TIM is one of the 4 mobile operators. Although Telecom Italia was bought by Telefonica in Europe, TIM in Brazil is obliged to remain separate in all operational and marketing aspects from Vivo.

Mexican group Telmex owns mobile operator Claro, fixed and satellite services company Embratel and Pay-TV operator Net, and has become a strong converged services provider.

Prepaid phones make up 82% of the market, a proportion that is currently stable. The increase in mobile customers is mainly amongst the C and D categories and younger age groups, leading to low ARPU. Income from data transmission is low compared to Europe and Japan. SMS messaging is relatively uncommon.

All phones are now either GSM or 3G. 3G networks were rolled out in 2008 and by March 2011, there were 23m 3G accesses in use, up from 16.8m in September 2010.

Digital television, which will be universal within 10 years, has been operational for 3 years in the ISDB-T format.

Internet Access and Broadband

Over 67m Brazilians have regular access to the internet. There were 13.8m broadband internet accesses by December 2010, of which nearly 9m were ADSL. Cheaper computers thanks to tax reductions have helped with internet expansion although service costs continue to be very high in Brazil. The same applies to Pay-TV which had 10.2m customers by February 2011, up from 9.4m in October 2010.

The main providers of broadband are Oi, Net and Telefonica, with 80% of the market between them.

A national broadband plan has been launched by the government which proposes to iron out market anomalies such as excessively high prices, monopolistic activities and unfair competitive practices. The government intends to provide a high-speed internet service to all Brazilians at a price of between R$15 and R$35 per month. The Ministry of Communications expects to invest R$79bn in the project.

3G

The focus in 2011 for telecommunications will be on 3G expansion led by sales of new handsets and investment in 3G infra-structure.

3G networks have been set up by Nokia-Siemens, Ericsson, Huawei, and ZTE. Local manufacturers such as Ericsson, Nokia-Siemens and Motorola, Alcatel-Lucent, LG, Cisco, NEC, Huawei and ZTE are also the major importers of telecommunications equipment.

Factories have been set up with loan incentives from BNDES (Brazilian Development Bank) and tax incentives. A wide range of equipment is made locally, including accessories, cables, connectors, racks, mobiles, public telephones and PABX, modems, multiplexers, optical technology and software.

Network equipment is either imported or assembled locally. Local manufacturers are coming under increasing pressure from the rising value of the Real, which has reached R$1.57 to the US$ in April 2011.

Regulation

Any telecommunications product supplied into the operators has to be approved by Anatel, the regulatory body: www.anatel.org.br.

Suppliers must have a Brazilian representative to guarantee after-sales service. A partner in the market is useful to negotiate local market difficulties such as long lead times to contract, high taxation (40% of the consumer's bill is tax), bureaucracy and, in the case of mobile applications, a relatively low level of revenue passed on by operators.

Chapter 27: Brazil FPSO's in the Gulf of Mexico

Floating and Production, Storing and Offloading ships have been developed over a 30 year period by Petrobras and are now common on the Pre SALT and Campos basin oil fields. Two of the main advantage of these very large ships is that they can store oil, which is very useful where there is no pipeline and they can get out of the way of inclement weather. Certainly they have a limit in terms of capacity, as one will eventually fill anything up but for the Gulf of Mexico, which has very deep areas where there are no pipelines and some pretty horrible hurricanes. Most hurricane seasons see the suspension of oil production and the destruction of many platforms, which when you have thousands in operation is a risky and expensive business.

One of the latest ships being operated by Petrobras is the BW Pioneer, which can drill to a depth of 2,500 m, a record for this type of drilling platform and can process up to 80,000 barrels per day. This system of oil production requires two sets of flexible connecting pipe work, one that connects the rigid vertical pipes to the FPSO and then another set that connects the FBSO to the shuttle tankers that take the oil to the land based refinery. Two of the many challenges involved with flexible oil lines are how the pipes are connected and disconnected, whilst at the same time dealing the high pressure and the other is mooring the top of the vertical risers when not connected to the FPSO.

A whole set of critical developments, which are some of the reasons why oil and gas technology developed in the Brazilian oil fields are being exported around the world and we will be seeing more and more exported around the world.

Chapter 28: Challenges of Transparency

As some people will know President Dilma Rousseff has, since she took over from President Lula in November 2010, suffered the resignation of three ministers Antonio Palocci (Home Affairs), Alfredo Nascimento (Transport) and Wagner Rossi (Agriculture) due to alleged corruption. There have also been a number of other high officials who have also resigned.

At the swearing in of the new Minister for Agriculture Mendes Ribeiro, Presidente Rousseff said "that it was her duty to see an end to the impunity which shelters many of those accused of involvement in corruption practices and we will punish all abuses and excesses." It appears that the President is taking a much harder line on corruption than her predecessors, but runs the political risk of alienating some of her political support in Congress.

The challenge though with this sort of social change is the relationship between corruption, transparency, the handling of political power and the distribution of wealth. These items have been the bogey men through history for all countries and as you might imagine some countries are worse than others. What some people may not know is that all signatories to the OCED have since 2002 been party to the International Transparency ratings list.

The interesting thing is that the Scandinavian countries are way out ahead, the Antipodes are at the top with some of Europe, the UK is above the US and France but the BRICS are quite a way down and President Roussseff wants to improve their position as Brazil begins to take a more important place on the world stage.

Certainly for the UK this is a bit of a wake-up call and certainly it is great that Brazil is doing something about it.

Chapter 29: Doing Business in Rio de Janeiro

Rio is a huge city with a lot of great business opportunities and it is also one of the most beautiful cities on Earth. Talk about the best of both worlds! Rio will not only be one of the host cities for the 2014 World Cup but it will also host the 2016 Olympic Games. Needless to say, there is a lot going on in that city. Like in other cities in Brazil, a lot of the opportunities are related to hospitality, tourism, infrastructure and transportation. Aside from that, one other area that is very attractive is oil and energy.

Cariocas (as people from Rio are called) are very warm and easy to work with. They are much more casual in how they talk and approach business as a whole. Don't ever try to compare Rio to Sao Paulo because you will be in for a surprise. Even though cariocas are very professional they tend to be much more laid back and easy going than business people from Sao Paulo. You can notice this as soon as you talk to a carioca. You don't need to be Brazilian to notice the difference. The way they move and their mannerisms will show you right away what they consider important or not. Cariocas are not very politically correct but don't take this as them trying to be rude or disrespectful. To them, life and business should be simple and that's how they do things. As most Brazilians, they value relationships. A lot of business is done outside of the office. Lunches and happy hours are more common especially because it's easier to leave the office and sit in nice places with a beautiful beach view. Who wouldn't want to do that?

As far as dress code goes, cariocas are much more casual than business people in Sao Paulo. Business casual is safe but I always advise anyone to go a little more formal for the first meeting. That will give you the opportunity to feel the place and the people you will be working with. It is more common to see jeans in Rio but always dress it up with a jacket. There are certain businesses that do require suits and those would be; law firms, investment companies and government entities. If you have any questions regarding dress code, make sure to reach out to the company you will be visiting and ask. Always better to be on the safe side.

Downtown Rio de Janeiro

Safety is still a topic of concern for many foreigners visiting Rio. Know that things have gotten much better and the city is much safer. As you would in any big city, be aware of your surroundings. There are areas where you can walk around without a problem but if you go downtown, for example, make sure to hold your belongings close to you and avoid areas with less foot traffic. In turn, areas with a lot of foot traffic can become dangerous if you are not paying attention. Robberies can happen and very fast. The key here is to walk with confidence and not looking around mesmerized by what you see.

As far as taxis, it's always safer to have a number for one you can call. To get one on the street, make sure the taxi driver has his/her credentials on the front view mirror. Most taxis in Rio are yellow with blue stripes along the sides. I myself took many taxis on the street and had no issues. If a driver wants to get you to pay a fixed price, do not go for it. Have them run the meter and pay what the route is worth. Be mindful that most taxis do not take credit cards so always have some cash with you.

One cannot go to Rio without experiencing the city, its natural beauty and its culture. Don't think what you see on TV is all Rio is about. Yes, there are beautiful beaches but there is a lot more.

Chapter 30: Doing Business in Belo Horizonte, Brazil

Belo Horizonte is the 5th largest city in Brazil in terms of population with about 2.3 million people. It is also one of the 2014 World Cup host cities. Even though this is a very large city, Belo Horizonte manages to maintain its small town feel. It is hard to compare Belo Horizonte to cities like São Paulo or Rio de Janeiro. Mineiros, as people from Minas Gerais are called, are very warm and hospitable. If you go there, you will notice a very distinguished accent. It's amazing how this city is so close to São Paulo, for example, and how the accent can be so different.

When it comes to business, mineiros are really into building relationships with their partners, clients and or counterparts. Expect to spend a lot more time compared to other cities in Brazil building a trustworthy relationship enough to really do business. This can be very cumbersome and frustrating to someone who wants to meet deadlines and get things done. Know beforehand that things won't move quickly. You will need to spend a lot of time meeting, dining, and creating chemistry with your partner from Minas. If there is not a good relationship, the deal will probably not materialize. Even to this day it is common to have verbal agreements amongst business partners. Of course, both ends eventually end up creating a contract but that will come much later.

If you are concerned about time, know that mineiros tend to run late. Yes, Brazilians are famous for not being the most punctual people in the world but even inside Brazil the punctuality goes from state to state. In Belo Horizonte or any other city in Minas Gerais, however, it is common for meetings to start 20-40 minutes late. When doing business there I would highly advise one to be flexible and exercise their patience. My suggestion is always to not schedule meetings back-to-back and for lunch meetings, make sure to allow yourself up to 3 hours, just in case.

Safety is not as big of an issue there as it is in Sao Paulo or Rio de Janeiro. Being it a big city, of course incidents happen but as long as you exercise caution and be aware of your surroundings, you should be ok. The city has seen an increase in foreign investment and in foreign workers, especially in IT. There is also lot of construction going on in the city right now as it is getting ready for the 2014 World Cup.

A lot of improvements in infrastructure and transportation are being made. As in all other 11 host cities, the stadium is under renovation and it should be ready in December of 2012. There is not one place you go in that city where you will not see some sort of construction.

One concern, which can be seen as an opportunity, is the lack of hotels. Some are being built but the local population is hesitant and concerned that the city may not have enough rooms to support all the tourists coming for the games. With two years to go the city really needs to ramp up on construction of new hotels and even hostels and furnished condos. If you are looking for a place to stay, I would suggest Savassi which is a very nice and safe area. Of course your location depends on where you will be going but if you choose to stay in an area not so close to where you are doing business, you can expect to spend from 15 – 30 min by taxi. Traffic is heavy during rush hour but aside from that, things move pretty smoothly.

If you have to do business in Belo Horizonte or with people from there you will be pleasantly surprised as to how warm and willing to help people are. Remember to take things a bit slowly and invest on your networking and relationship building. I would also highly recommend attending events organized by the American Chamber of Commerce (AmCham) Even though there is "American" in the name, this chamber is mainly a good place for networking with people from every industry. If you don't know where to start or how to meet the most influential people in Belo Horizonte, I would definitely start there.

When it comes to life outside the office, be ready to experience the cuisine from Minas which is very rich and simply delicious. Belo Horizonte is also known for having the largest number of bars in Brazil. Most of these bars have outside seating and you can have great appetizers while also enjoying the nice weather while seating outside. I also recommend you visit Lagoa da Pampulha which is a very nice lake with beautiful views and surrounded by great restaurants and bars.

Chapter 31: Doing Business in São Paulo, Brazil

If you are considering doing business in Brazil or have already started, chances are you will go to São Paulo. The number one concern when going to that city is safety but I am here to tell you not to believe everything you see in the news. Like any other big city in the world, São Paulo has its safety issues but nothing different from New York, for example. Of course, be aware of your surroundings and follow some of my tips when it comes to staying safe in Brazil.

Paulistanos (how people from the city are called) are great to work with. They are usually on time and it's very easy to do business in English. My own experience this time has been extremely positive in that all my appointments started exactly at the right time. Meetings can run long but that's expected when working with Brazilians. It's not common for people to go straight to the point but you can feel more comfortable doing that in São Paulo. I would recommend a 15 minute ice breaker just trying to get to know the person and then you can talk business.

The city in itself is much more prepared than other cities in Brazil to receive foreigners and no matter where you go, you will hear not only English but a lot of different languages. Some nicer restaurants have menus in English and those are usually the places where you see a lot of business people. Deals are not closed in restaurants but they are definitely celebrated there. And remember, if you are doing business in São Paulo, take advantage of the large array of restaurants. The city offers incredible gastronomy experiences. Be prepared to spend a lot of money but think of this as an investment as you take your clients and/or Brazilian counterparts out. Brazilians like to impress and they appreciate being impressed. For a nice dinner expect to spend $150-$200/person. If you add a bottle of wine then you can raise this per person value by a lot.

Now, the one thing in São Paulo that can be very difficult to deal with is traffic. This is a very large city and depending on where you are, you can spend at least 40 minutes in the car trying to get to another location, no matter the time of the day. Plan ahead and know exactly where you are and where you need to go. If you ask anyone how long you need to get to a certain location, add 30 more minutes just to be on the safe side. If you are like me, you will be taking taxis a lot. One good option may be to hire the driver for the day and pay about R$300/day ($160.) With this the driver can take you from one place to the next and you don't have to worry about flagging taxis on the street, which I don't recommend. Finding taxi drivers who speak English can be a challenge but some do. I found one who spoke perfect English and because of this he charged R$500/day ($260) to be at a client's disposal. Completely worth it.

Paulistanos are very business-oriented and professional. They can be more straight-forward and to the point, a good thing for any foreigner trying to meet milestones and deadlines. For all the businesswomen out there like me, expect to be dealing with a lot of men. This is still a man's world. Women are respected and the number of women in upper management has been growing. However, it's still a very low number compared to men. You will see more women in Sao Paulo doing business, which is great.

Even if you are doing business in São Paulo, try to take time to know the city. It has so much to offer in every aspect. Whatever you are in the mood for, you will find in that city. The best restaurants from every type of cuisine are there. Brazilians love bars and clubs. If you have the opportunity to go to some, you will not be disappointed. I had the opportunity to go on a pub crawl and it was an incredible experience. You will probably hear that Paulistanos can be a little cold compared to the rest of Brazilians but that's not true. If you are open to a great experience, they will not only be great business partners but they will also show you a great time.

Chapter 32: Tips for a Successful Business Trip to Brazil

As I prepare to travel once again to Brazil, I decided to share with you some tips that will definitely help you get the most out of your business trip to that country. Since you won't be doing business 24 hours a day (at least I hope not) I will also include some tips for out of the office activities. Enjoy!

Arrange your meetings prior to leaving your home country

This goes without saying but you will find that when you reach out to many Brazilians they will simply say "Let's definitely meet. Give me a call or e-mail me when you get here and we will arrange something." Red flag. Try as best as you can to have a time and location set up ahead of time. Brazilians are very flexible and this may work for some but your goal is to have meetings scheduled before you get on the plane. Follow up with an e-mail politely saying that your schedule is filling up and you would rather have a time, date and location in place so you can make sure the meeting will happen.

Confirm your appointments a few days prior to the meeting

You may have everything scheduled and you are ready to go. Not so fast. Make sure to confirm all your appointments and if there are any changes, adjust your schedule accordingly. It never hurts to keep the communication flowing. Many times things will happen and your Brazilian counterparts may not communicate changes to you. Do your follow-ups and if something falls through, try to either schedule something else or use the extra time to network. Again, the more networking you do, the more successful you will be.

Do not book meetings back-to-back

My advice to you is to book one meeting in the morning and one in the afternoon. Keep in mind that things can run late and a morning meeting may turn into a lunch. Try not to do too much in one day. In Brazil it's all about relationship building and relaxing. Prepare to spend at least 2 to 3 hours during lunch. If you have a meeting starting at 10am, chances are you could end up stretching that into a lunch. Same applies to afternoon meetings. Next thing you know you may be going to a happy hour. To be on the safe side, schedule two and not more than three meetings a day. Leave some wiggle room between meetings to account for traffic and for icebreakers that may take the time of the entire meeting.

Plan restaurant reservations ahead of time

A lot of the nicest restaurants in Brazil not only require reservation but you need to have them made many times weeks ahead of time. The nicer the restaurant, the longer the waiting period. Plan ahead. And remember, this is not the time to spare expense with clients or prospects. Do your homework and be ready to treat your Brazilian counterparts well. The one who invites, pays.

Learn as much Portuguese as you can

In an ideal world you would speak fluent Portuguese but we all know how realistic that goal is. If you are not taking classes, start now. Most business people in Brazil speak English so you should be good on that front. However, if you want to truly be successful you need to speak the language. At least enough for you to get by at first. Not only will this show Brazilians you are serious about doing business with them but you will have to rely on translators, interpreters and on working only with people who speak English.

Pack your patience

Business in Brazil is a "dance" so be prepared to be flexible and patient. Deadlines and milestones may not be met at the speed you expect. Know this beforehand and your level of frustration will be minimized. As I have said many times before, doing business in Brazil is a social interaction so expect to have a few more meetings than you would in your home country before you get something accomplished. Brazilians may not be ready to work on your timeline and if you are the one interested in doing business with them, the best advice I can give you is to follow their lead. There are ways you can get what you want but maybe not in the way you are used to.

Have fun

I don't know one person who goes to Brazil for business and doesn't spend any time outside the office. Don't avoid social interactions with your prospects, partners, and possible future employees. Spend time with the people will be working with. They will appreciate your willingness to enjoy their company and you will learn a lot about them and about the local culture. How can you go to a country like Brazil and expect to not have fun, right? Enjoy your time there and be sure that you may get more results out of some outings than out of a meeting in an office. Also, while you are there, try to visit not only touristic attractions but also museums, national libraries, parks and outside events. Doing business in Brazil is about experiencing the country as well. I am sure you will enjoy this part.

After spending a month in Brazil doing business and enjoying some vacation I am now more than ever convinced that to be successful there you need to be flexible and spontaneous. One can have the best market entry strategy, the best strategic planning in place and the best products and/or services but if you don't know how to deal with the Brazilian business culture, all of the above don't mean a thing. I say this from experience.

Being in Brazil for a long period of time gave me a chance to go understand how to do business in Brazil and realize that it's not all about the bottom line… it's about how you get there. Every meeting I had took a different course than what I had expected and every encounter turned into an event. Don't get me wrong, I loved it! Last week I had a meeting at 10am that was supposed to last an hour. Well, I was only able to leave after 1:30pm. What's the lesson here? Do not plan meetings back-to-back. You never know if the meeting will turn into a lunch where you will be able to meet other partners and clients or simply deepen the relationship you already have.

I also did a presentation on how to work with Americans at the American Chamber of Commerce in Brasilia and everything started on time. The presentation went great and I made great contacts. Do you think I was done after my seminar was over? Of course not. I ended up being invited to meet the head of the International Affairs Committee which in turn ended up becoming a lunch at a restaurant followed by coffee at a different location. Long story short, I started my day at 8:30am and ended it at 4:30pm. Again, had I not been flexible and available, I would not have made the contacts I did.

My point? Do have all your strategies and numbers in place but don't forget that the most important thing in Brazil when doing business is relationship building. My advice to anyone going there is to schedule one or two meetings max a day. Go with the flow and you will be surprised how much more you will get done. Allow yourself to become part of the culture and don't be so frustrated and uptight that things seem to be taking longer than you expected. Be flexible. Be spontaneous. Have coffee. Have lunch. Enjoy a nice bottle of wine and learn about your business partners. You will be glad you did.

Chapter 33: Five Questions you should Answer before Doing Business in Brazil

The more I interact with people, who want to do business in Brazil, the more I have been asking this question: "why do you want to do business there"? I have had a few people ask me to give them some ideas as to what they should do. You may not be surprised by that, but I am every time, especially when there is no answer. Then I realized a lot of people are simply eager to get on the Brazil bandwagon that they don't really take the time to figure out why and how they will get there. All they know is that they want to do business in that country because that is where the money is. Let's pause for a second.

For anyone thinking about doing business in Brazil, here are a few questions you should ask yourself:

1) Is Brazil a good market for my services or products?

This should be one of the first questions you should ask yourself. Just because Brazil has been in the spotlight and has done fairly well, it doesn't necessarily mean there is a market for you. Look at your offerings and think how they could be best used in a country like Brazil. Maybe you will have to change or adapt your services/products a little to best fit the market. If you are lucky, you don't. Spend some time thinking about the pros and cons as well as the opportunities and threats. Who knows? Maybe you need to come up with a slightly different business model. I have seen so many companies going to Brazil thinking their product or service is unique and will thrive in Brazil only to realize that there is no market or that the competition is so fierce that they can't compete with the local companies. What do you have to offer that will stand out from the local offerings? How can you differentiate yourself from what's already there? Better yet, how can you adapt your business model to fit the needs of Brazilians? Think about that. If you can't answer this question, you may not be ready to go there quite yet.

2) What kind of research do I need to do to get started?

Now that you already know why you want to do business in Brazil you should do a lot of research. You already know that but it doesn't hurt to emphasize this step. Don't just rely on research from your home country. Make sure to work with good professionals and build good connections in Brazil. Try to get a perspective as an outsider and as an insider. What are the commonalities? Many times the information you receive in your home country about Brazil may be a bit skewed. Talk to Brazilians as well and make your own judgement as to what makes sense for you and your company. Join chambers of commerce or reach out to the local Brazilian communities in your area. Read good Brazilian publications online and good international business publications in your home country. Do you see a difference in how the news is portrayed? There is always a bias so try to absorb as much information from both sides so you can have the best possible information. Never rely on one source. Big mistake.

3) What kind of professionals should I surround myself with to be successful?

Don't think for a second you can do this alone. You will need to surround yourself with great international lawyers, international accountants, cross-cultural consultants and other international business professionals who can help bridge the gap between the two countries and cultures. You will also need to have good local partners because in Brazil it's all about who you know. If you have a good team, your business will thrive. Spare no expense here because if you try to do this alone or try to do this your way, you will run the risk of having to start over or fix something that was broken along the way. Yes, Brazil can be a complex country to work with but not if you have the right people working with and for you.

4) What do I know about Brazilians and their country?

A lot of people disregard this step all together. They think about the money and they don't really take the time to learn about the country, its people and its culture. Many business people see Brazil as just another Latin country and since they have done business with Latin countries before, why should this be different? You are in for a big surprise. Yes, Brazil shares many similarities with the Spanish-speaking countries but let me tell you, Brazil is a different beast. Inside Brazil there are many different cultures and many different ways of doing business. You can't assume Recife is the same as Sao Paulo or that Rio de Janeiro is the same as Rio Grande do Sul. Understanding the culture, knowing about the country and knowing how the people behave will be your key to success. I hear business people say that they are tired of spending so much time wining, dining, and wasting time talking about other things other than business. Well, if you know anything about the Brazilian culture, none of this is a waste of time. Visit Brazil, learn about the culture and live the culture as much as feasibly possible. Spend time with people and try to find out what they care about as a nation. This will be a very powerful tool as you enter this market. To make things even easier, work with someone who can help you and your team understand the culture and the language. If you find someone who understands both cultures, even better.

5) What region in Brazil would my products or services be more needed?

In a way this step could be in the "research" area however, once you have decided to go into Brazil you will need to determine where in Brazil your offerings will give you the biggest ROI. 80% of businesses these days are done in Sao Paulo. Does it mean you should go there? Maybe, but not necessarily. The northeast of Brazil is an area that investors should look into, especially in agri-business, tourism, hospitality, and infrastructure. Four cities in the northeast will host the 2014 World Cup games (Recife, Salvador, Natal, and Fortaleza.) Manaus in the north will also be a host city. Depending on your offerings you may want to explore these areas. What about the south of Brazil? Porto Alegre and Curitiba will also host the 2014 World Cup games and these areas are much more developed than the north in many areas. Since the games will be in June, these two cities will be pretty cold. Could this offer an opportunity for you? Remember, it will be winter season in Brazil when the games happen. Does that mean something to you? In cities like Curitiba and Porto Alegre where the temperature can drop to below freezing levels, is there something that you could offer that maybe Brazilians don't? Food for thought. Try to think outside the box and always take into account the region you are going into. Winter in the south means cold, whereas winter in the north means rain.

If you can answer all five questions above, you can trust that you are on the right path to having a successful business in Brazil. In the end, you will have fun learning about this market and discovering all the amazing opportunities that are out there and have not yet been untapped. Roll up your sleeves and good luck!

Chapter 34: Conclusion

Brazil is not considered an easy country to do business with for several reasons. The local language is Portuguese, and many Brazilians do not speak English. It is recommended therefore that the need for an interpreter is assessed when you come to the market to meet prospects.

The market is still subject to high import duties and various taxes that are likely to at least double the FOB price of a product arriving at the customer (distributor) in Brazil. Customs documents must be 100% correct to avoid unpleasant situations with customs. For this reason, it is essential to deal with a representative who knows the procedures and has good local contacts.

Brazil is a price-orientated market but niches are available to quality products as long as they have good service, trained technicians and support from the supplier. Brazilians are well-informed business people, on both domestic and international matters. Business sometimes takes time, as the culture requires that business relationships are based on getting to know your partners over a period of time. It is wise to approach Brazil with a medium to long term strategy.

As it is a large and very diverse country, it is important to consider local companies that have knowledge of the markets you wish to approach. If you approach Brazil as a whole, keep your options open when giving exclusivity contracts to companies.

Clearly set out the boundaries for distributors when taking a regional approach.

Brazilians are very sociable and like to meet new business partners before signing any deal. Once you have reached a point where you believe that the market is receptive to your products, we recommend that you visit the market preferably within three months. If a longer period passes before your visit, we recommend that you get an update done on the contacts given, before your visiting programme is set up. It is usually necessary to visit the market at least annually to best develop business.

Useful Brazilian Portuguese phrases
- good morning, afternoon, Bom dia, boa tarde,
- evening/night boa noite
- nice to meet you muito prazer
- it's OK, no problem tudo bem, sem problema
- yesterday, today, tomorrow ontem, hoje, amanhã
- Hello! Oi! Hi!,
- how are you? como vai/como está?
- please por favor
- thank you obrigado (for men)
- thank you obrigada (for women)
- you're welcome de nada
- I'm sorry me desculpe
- excuse me com licença
- coffee café
- milk leite
- tea chá

- water água
- bye, see you soon tchau, até logo
- one, two, three, four, five um, dois, três, quatro, cinco
- toilet banheiro